STUDIES

IN THE

SOCIAL ASPECTS

OF THE

DEPRESSION

Studies in the Social Aspects of the Depression

Advisory Editor: *ALEX BASKIN*

State University of New York at Stony Brook

RESEARCH MEMORANDUM ON RELIGION IN THE DEPRESSION

By SAMUEL C. KINCHELOE

ARNO PRESS
A NEW YORK TIMES COMPANY

Reprint Edition 1972 by Arno Press Inc.

Reprinted from a copy in The Newark Public Library

LC# 71-162843
ISBN 0-405-00846-5

Studies in the Social Aspects of the Depression
ISBN for complete set: 0-405-00840-6
See last pages of this volume for titles.

Manufactured in the United States of America

Preface to the New Edition

The winds of change whipped through America in the early years of the Depression. In response to a survey made of twenty thousand Protestant ministers in 1934, nearly one-third indicated their preference for socialism as a humane and viable way of life. One cannot help, in light of these astonishing figures, but be reminded of Marx's admonition to the proletarians of his day that religion was the opiate of the working class and that its servants fostered views antithetical to those of the socialist movement. This radical turn of the clergy, however, is not difficult to understand if one remembers that unemployment had reached historic depths and that all the words of encouragement which had echoed through the public ear for several years were to no avail.

The religious response to the economic situation varied with place and sect. Some viewed the cataclysmic events which began with the Wall Street debacle as a sign from an angered and wrathful God giving voice to His discontent in an eloquently dramatic and effective way. Too long had man coveted the material world and too long had he trod the secular road. In the minds of some zealous preachers, the Depression augured well for religion. Those who had strayed would now return to the faith of their fathers. In other church circles there was a deep and abiding concern for the plight of the jobless and their families. Religious organizations were among the first to respond to the call of the needy. Bread lines formed outside missions and church-supported soup kitchens filled many an empty stomach. The hungry queued up four and five abreast in lines that stretched for blocks. The procession was slow and ponderous. The spirit of the Social Gospel which had thrived in the closing decades of the nineteenth century was awakened in the 1930's, but these philanthropic efforts buckled beneath the crush of an overwhelming response. The economic crisis, which weighed so heavily on the millions of unemployed, reflected itself in the diminished gifts and charitable offerings made to the various denominations.

Those who dreamed of a massive return to the church and a period of revival were to be disappointed. Mr. Kincheloe, in this study, discusses church membership and attendance and graphically discloses the downward trend of both. The salaries of the churchmen reflected the general economic decline and, as might be expected, were cut sharply. In some rural communities, the faithful worshipped without the benefit of paid clergy or ordained ministers.

In examining the response of a number of religious bodies, Mr. Kincheloe has described clearly and succinctly the various plans put forth. The Security Program of the Church of Jesus Christ of Latter Day Saints (Mormons) aimed at establishing the family as a self-sustaining and supporting unit. As part of this endeavor, the church made labor surveys, gathered food, fuel and clothing for its members, established cooperatives, and organized canning and recreational units.

The religious impulse has survived the test of time and the turbulence of the 1930's. We are again living in an era of pronounced change where many of our moral values and manners are being tested and abrogated. New modes of worship are being introduced. Clerics now make the news because they stand in the vanguard of social thought and social consciousness. The winds of change whipped through America in the early years of the Depression. They are gaining fresh momentum in the decade of the seventies.

Alex Baskin
Stony Brook, New York, 1971

BULLETIN 33

1937

RESEARCH MEMORANDUM ON RELIGION IN THE DEPRESSION

By SAMUEL C. KINCHELOE

Associate Professor of the Sociology of Religion

The Chicago Theological Seminary

PREPARED UNDER THE DIRECTION OF THE COMMITTEE ON STUDIES IN SOCIAL ASPECTS OF THE DEPRESSION

SOCIAL SCIENCE RESEARCH COUNCIL

230 PARK AVENUE NEW YORK NY

The Social Science Research Council was organized in 1923 and formally incorporated in 1924, composed of representatives chosen from the seven constituent societies and from time to time from related disciplines such as law, geography, psychiatry, medicine, and others. It is the purpose of the Council to plan, foster, promote, and develop research in the social field.

CONSTITUENT ORGANIZATIONS

American Anthropological Association

American Economic Association

American Historical Association

American Political Science Association

American Psychological Association

American Sociological Society

American Statistical Association

FOREWORD

By the Committee on Studies in Social Aspects of the Depression

THIS monograph on research pertaining to religion in the depression is one of a series of thirteen sponsored by the Social Science Research Council to stimulate the study of depression effects on various social institutions. The full list of titles is on page ii.

The depression of the early 1930's was like the explosion of a bomb dropped in the midst of society. All major social institutions, such as the government, family, church, and school, obviously were profoundly affected and the repercussions were so far reaching that scarcely any type of human activity was untouched.

It would be valuable to have assembled the vast record of influence of this economic depression on society. Such a record would constitute an especially important preparation for meeting the shock of the next depression, if and when it comes. The facts about the impact of the depression on social life have been only partially recorded. Theories must be discussed and explored now, if much of the information to test them is not to be lost amid ephemeral sources.

The field is so broad that selection has been necessary. In keeping with its mandate from the Social Science Research Council, the Committee sponsored no studies of an exclusively economic or political nature. The subjects chosen for inclusion were limited in number by resources. The final selection was made by the Committee from a much larger number of proposed subjects, on the basis of social importance and available personnel.

Although the monographs clearly reveal a uniformity of goal, they differ in the manner in which the various authors sought to attain that goal. This is a consequence of the Committee's belief that the promotion of research could best be served by not imposing rigid restrictions on the organization of materials by the contributors. It is felt that the encouraged freedom in approach and organization has resulted in the enrichment of the individual reports and of the series as a whole.

A common goal without rigidity in procedure was secured by requesting each author to examine critically the literature on the depression for the purpose of locating existing data and interpretations already reasonably well established, of discovering the more serious inadequacies in information, and of formulating research problems feasible for study. He was not expected to do this research himself. Nor was he expected to compile a full and systematically treated record of the depression as experienced in his field. Nevertheless, in indicating the new research which is needed, the writers found it necessary to report to some extent on what is known. These volumes actually contain much information on the social influences of the depression, in addition to their analyses of pressing research questions.

The undertaking was under the staff direction of Dr. Samuel A. Stouffer, who worked under the restrictions of a short time limit, in order that prompt publication might be assured. He was assisted by Mr. Philip M. Hauser and Mr. A. J. Jaffe. The Committee wishes to express appreciation to authors, who contributed their time and effort without remuneration, and to the many other individuals who generously lent aid and materials.

William F. Ogburn Chairman
Shelby M. Harrison
Malcolm M. Willey

PREFACE

RELIGION makes its basic changes slowly. The big question to determine is that of the degree to which the changes occurring during a time of depression were already under way and were simply speeded up or retarded by the depression, and to what extent the depression created situations so different that new factors began their work. In many cases the old trends probably continued, but were influenced by conditions due to the depression. An effort is made to analyze some of the situations and conditions under which the depression may have brought about significant changes in the field of religion, and to outline some of the problems on which we need further study.

While some attention is given in this monograph to religion as broadly interpreted, the limitations of data and the need of concentrating research at points where research is feasible require that the principal consideration be given to the church as an institution.

The term "church" is used to include all worshipping religious organizations—Catholic, Protestant, and Jewish. When the term "the church" is used, it is used in the same sense in which one uses the term "the school," "the family," "the state," etc.

Most of the illustrations and data refer to Protestant churches. The writer has had the helpful counsel of Roman Catholic priests and Jewish rabbis, but feels that the limitations of his own experience are such that he could not give, in the limited time available, adequate treatment of these groups. It is hoped that many of the ideas and concrete suggestions here presented will interest Catholic and Jewish research workers, even if important modifications would need to be made in suggestions which in their present form are more strictly applicable to Protestant groups.

The writer is indebted to many members of the Chicago Theological Seminary and of the University of Chicago faculty, and to members of the Chicago Congregational Union staff. He is especially indebted to Professor Arthur E. Holt with whom he has shared a seminar on urban life. He wishes to thank particularly the following members of the seminar: John Berry, Ralph Cummins, Paul Dickey, Marion Giersbach, Ellen Tweedy Greene, Shirley Greene, Marilee Kone, Margaret Medland, Audrey Peterson, Gilbert K. Robinson, P. M. Titus, Lewis Troyer, and Sharvy Umbeck. For reading parts of the manuscript and giving criticism and suggestions he wishes to thank Edwin E. Aubrey, William Clayton Bower, Ernest Graham Guthrie, Arthur Cushman McGiffert, Jr., and Warren S. Thompson. To numerous ministers, church administrators, and sociologists in many states he wishes to make acknowledgment for answering a large number of letters and for contributing many helpful insights.

Samuel C. Kincheloe

CONTENTS

		PAGE
	FOREWORD	v
	PREFACE	vii
I	CHURCH MEMBERSHIP AND ATTENDANCE	1
II	CHURCH FINANCES	17
III	THE CLERGY	31
IV	SECULARIZATION: GENERAL CONSIDERATIONS	45
V	THE MESSAGE	59
VI	PROGRAM AND ACTIVITIES	89
	APPENDIX A REGIONAL AND RURAL VARIATIONS	117
	APPENDIX B THE STUDY OF THE LOCAL CHURCH IN THE DEPRESSION	138
	APPENDIX C THE CIVIC FUNCTIONS OF THE PARISH IN QUEBEC	146
	INDEX	149

Chapter I

Church Membership and Attendance

SOME religious leaders actually hailed the depression with rejoicing since they had the idea that previous depressions had "driven men to God" and felt that the time was overdue for men again to be reminded of the need to let the spiritual dominate the materialistic order. A sermon was preached in the Chicago area[1] which pointed to each of the great depressions and the revivalists who arose with them.[2] The preacher said:

> In connection with the depression of 1837-1841, I think of Lyman Beecher as a powerful leader in the religious movement which, during the years of the depression, swept through our country, with the result that Christians were quickened and strengthened, and great numbers of the unchurched experienced and professed conversion.
>
> In connection with the depression of 1857-1860 I think of Charles G. Finney . . . thousands believed and were added to the church.
>
> In connection with the depression of 1893 and thereafter I think of B. Fay Mills and J. Wilbur Chapman.
>
> This concurrence between commercial crises and consequent depressions in the past, on the one hand, and periods of spiritual revival, on the other hand, is something more than mere coincidence. There is a deep relation between the two classes of events. It appears to be this: when vast masses of men, as at present, encounter adversity, anxiety and perplexity, they lose confidence in themselves and, if properly led, turn to God.

The revival of 1858 came in the very parts of the country where the depression hit the hardest. It is said to have occurred "among the business and downtown clerical people of the cities

---

[1] Waldo, Alfred F. Pamphlet, privately printed at launching of Chicago United Spiritual Program. Riverside Presbyterian Church. October 11, 1931

[2] See Chapter VI, of this monograph, on revivals and the depression.

and larger towns—classes not predisposed to idealistic or enthusiastic interpretation of religion."[3] The current writers of that day definitely related the revival to the depression.

Today the correspondence of the writer with ministers in all parts of the United States, clearly reveals an expectancy that men would be compelled to turn to religion.

Roger W. Babson takes the position that it is the lack of spirituality and the lack of the preaching of sacrifice which produces depressions. It is his theory that, in times of depression, the preaching of self-sacrifice turns people to religion and that the gains show during times of prosperity. People then become careless and church attendance and additions fall off. Mr. Babson, as chairman of the Commission on Church Attendance of the Congregational-Christian denomination, gave the following conclusions:[4]

1. Newton's Law of Action and Reaction applies to church attendance as to general business.
2. An upward surge of the national growth line always accompanies an increase in church attendance.
3. The years when church attendance and additions by confession reached the highest figures have been the years of greatest national growth as determined by business statistics.

Some writers insist, on the basis of general impression, that men have turned to a more spiritual interpretation of life. "A New Tide of Religion Sweeps Onward," is the heading of an article by P. W. Wilson.[5] He mentions many other factors aside from economic upheavals. He says:

A survey of religion throughout the world suggests three conclusions. First, since the turn of the century man has been subject to a wave of secularism which has reduced the volume of religious observance. Second, the tide has turned and there is a return of religious feeling. Third, the returning tide is affecting religious institutions: there is a revival of or-

[3] Gaddis, M. E. *Christian Perfectionism in America.* University of Chicago (Ph.D. thesis). 1929

[4] Babson, Roger W. *How to Increase Church Attendance.* New York: Fleming H. Revell Co. 1936. Opposite p. 160

[5] *N. Y. Sunday Times Magazine.* December 20, 1936. P. 3

ganized religion. . . . Fears of war, economic upheavals, the disintegration of families—these are among the reasons that are driving many people, by no means religious in profession, to the view that secular sanctions are not enough.

There are those who say that the emotional zeal which might have turned into the churches has been put into "near religious movements" such as zeal for Huey Long, the Townsend Movement, the New Deal, fervor for the Constitution, etc. Both President Roosevelt and Secretary Wallace have phrased speeches in religious ideology and terminology. The movements of Communism and Fascism in Europe have had many of the characteristics of religious movements.[6] Perhaps our emotional expressions are going into the so-called secular expressions of life which are nearer, or at least more practically related, to the issues which give rise to the sense of worry on the part of men.

These various positions raise the question which has been in many minds: What is the relationship of periods of depression and interest in religion?[7]

With all the concern that has been shown in the question of the relationship of religion to the economic order, one might expect to find studies which would throw light on the effects of depression periods on church membership and attendance. There has been much discussion on the relationship of Protestantism and Capitalism,[8] but there is no authoritative work either by church

[6] Spinka, Matthew. *Christianity Confronts Communism.* New York: Harper & Brothers. 1936

[7] See Landis, Benson Y: "The Church and Religious Activities." *American Journal of Sociology.* 40:780, 787 May 1935

[8] See Tawney, R. H. *Religion and the Rise of Capitalism.* New York: Harcourt, Brace & Co. 1926

Weber, Max. *The Protestant Ethic and the Spirit of Capitalism.* New York: Charles Scribner's Sons. 1930

Hobson, J. A. *The Relations of Religion and Economics.* New York: The Macmillan Co. 1931

Harkness, Georgia. *John Calvin: The Man and His Ethics.* New York: Holt. and Co. 1931

Robertson, H. M. *Aspects of the Rise of Economic Individualism: A Criticism of Max Weber and His School.* Cambridge, England: Cambridge University Press. 1933

historians or by sociologists and economists on the question of the relationship of interest in churches and the business cycle.

CHURCH MEMBERSHIP

The suggestion has been advanced by some clergymen that during the depression periods more persons became church members. This supposition might well serve as a working hypothesis for the investigation of church membership on different social and economic levels.

Church membership is a rough measure of the people's interest in, and desire for, association with the church as an institution. Theoretically we could expect an index of church membership (as the percentage of the population who are church members) to fluctuate either positively or negatively with the business cycle, if the latter influences the former in any given direction. If, however, a business depression increased membership in some groups and decreased it in others, it is possible that decreases would offset increases so that total membership figures would not fluctuate.

Unfortunately, total church membership data are so rough that they are not an adequate index of fluctuations in church interest. Large quantities of statistics are available as to the number of church members among the different denominations year by year, but a brief analysis of these data will reveal a number of deficiencies. In the first place the "church member" is a unit which varies widely in meaning between one denomination and another. Some groups include almost the total population as members—their requirements for membership are the barest minimum—while other groups use the term in a much narrower sense.[9] Among those groups in which membership is counted on a very broad and general basis, there can be no short term cyclical variations. Certain long time trends may be observable, but that is all.

[9] See *Census of Religious Bodies.* Washington: Bureau of the Census. 1926. I: 16

Among those religious groups in which membership is restricted—as for example, to "dues-paying" adults, in the case of certain Lutheran bodies—the concept of member is sufficiently clear and of such nature as to be of value in research. However, such data are frequently not regularly or correctly reported, or the amount of payment necessary for membership varies, or a different number of members of the family are included. These statistics, to be of greatest value, must include accurate reports from a large, constant group of reporting churches.

Another deficiency of the statistics lies in the fact that the methods of enumerating church membership appear to be very inaccurate. Very rarely is a thorough, accurate count ever taken; quite often the size of the membership in a given community is the preacher's guess or estimate. Many Roman Catholic churches have no membership rolls in the formal sense. An error that appears to be widespread among Protestant churches is the tendency to keep names on the rolls as members even when the individuals have died or have psychologically separated themselves from the church.[10]

Still another limitation of church membership figures is that they tell nothing whatsoever about the participation of the members in the life and activities of the church. Theoretically, there may be no variation in the number or percentage of church members between depression and prosperous years, and yet there may be great variation in members' participation in the church activities. This last cannot be inferred from published statistics of total membership and no denomination as yet (to this writer's knowledge) has attempted to classify its members according to the degree of their activities. This might be done, for example, on the basis of the number of services attended per unit of

[10] Information Service, December 12, 1936. New York: Department of Research and Education. Federal Council of the Churches of Christ in America. (See note regarding church statistics.)

time, on the number of other church programs attended or participated in per unit of time, or on the basis of gifts.[11]

As studies attempting to classify the members in this manner cannot now be made covering the predepression years and the years at the depth of the depression, it would seem that any data regarding the number of church members year by year among those groups in which almost everyone is included as a member are, for the purposes of this study, of little value. The effective body of actively interested members is so small in comparison with the total membership that major shifts in the number of vitally active members might take place without being reflected in the total church membership.

Another difficulty that arises when one attempts to translate total membership into an index of interest in the church is the biological factor. Certain denominations are concentrated in parts of the country where the birth rate is higher than in other parts. The church membership in these cases may grow from natural increase rather than from added interest.

Finally, even if we were to assume that the errors cancel each other and that the errors in one group are not very different from those in another, especially in the denominations of British American origin, the general total of church memberships is so much in the nature of a general average that significant regional or group variations are unnoticed.

In the country as a whole, on the basis of available statistics, there have not been significant changes in church membership during the depression. (See Figure 1.) There may, however, have been significant regional changes within the various denominational groupings.[12] (See Table I.) Let us examine some of the statistics (remembering, of course, there is likelihood of error). For example, the Southern Baptists have grown at a more

[11] Fry, C. Luther. *Diagnosing the Rural Church,* offers a study which sought to work out a methodology for studying church interest. Garden City: Doubleday, Doran & Co. 1924

[12] See Appendix A

rapid rate in recent years than have the Northern Baptists. The Southern Baptist, Southern Methodist, and Southern Presbyterian

FIGURE 1

CHURCH MEMBERSHIP FOR SELECTED DENOMINATIONS: UNITED STATES 1920-1935[a]

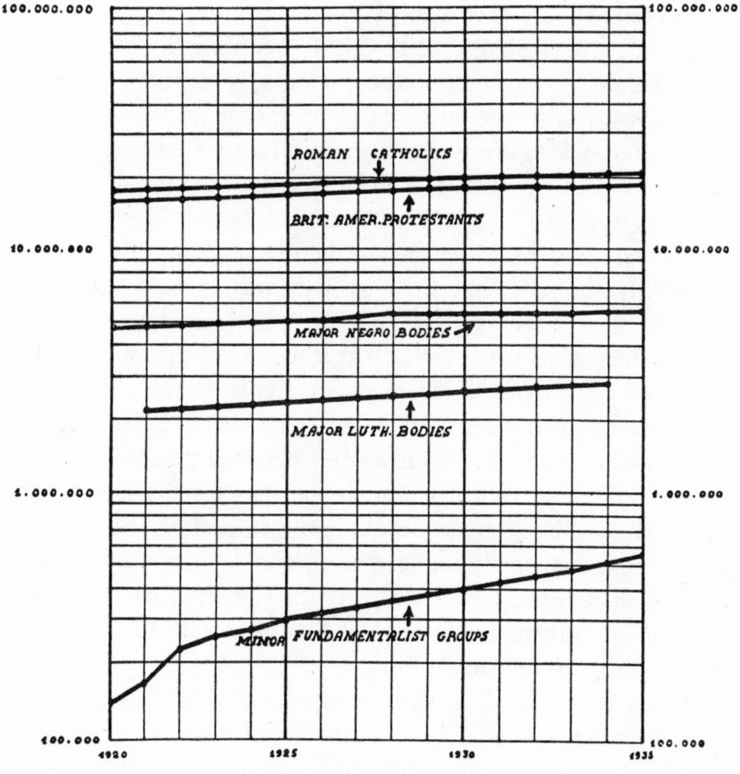

[a] Compiled from yearbooks of denominations indicated. For a list of statistical sources see *Yearbook of American Churches*, edited by H. C. Webber. Association Press, 1937

groups, combined, grew 15 per cent from 1920 to 1925 and 10 per cent from 1930 to 1935, while the Northern Baptist, Northern Methodist, and Northern Presbyterian groups grew 9 per cent from 1920 to 1925 and decreased 2 per cent from 1930 to 1935.[13] The Evangelical Synod of North America, which is a liberal group among those with Continental European origin, gained 15 per cent from 1930 to 1935. The Missouri Synod Lutheran, which is one of the most conservative of the Lutheran groups, gained 14 per cent from 1930 to 1935 and only 7 per cent from 1920 to 1925. (See Table I.)

No hasty conclusions dare be drawn regarding the effect of the type of theology or emotional expression, since there are many factors, especially the birth rate, operating in this situation. These yearbook figures suggest sharp increase in the percentage of members of the minor "fundamentalist groups" during the depression period. (See Figure 1.) Many of these upward trends were under way before the depression, and although it is commonly thought that their growth was greatly stimulated by it, the data show their rate of growth has been fairly constant during the period since 1925. It is to be noted that the number of persons belonging to these minor fundamentalist groups is very small in comparison with the other denominations; their actual numbers amount to only a few hundred thousand. An examination of the available church statistics reveals the relative constancy of the various denominational groups. Among the large established denominations one group does not readily make great gains over any other. However, it seems that the newer sects which have an adequate basis of appeal, may make inroads on the older established groups.

It will be a difficult, if not an impossible task, to secure adequate figures on the changes in membership in the Jewish groups, mainly because of the fact that individual synagogues do not report such data to a central office. Many Jewish rabbis give as their opinion[14] that membership in their own congregations has

[13] This last figure is not on the same basis as the others but is the nearest approximation which can be reached.

[14] In personal correspondence

TABLE I

PERCENTAGE INCREASE IN CHURCH MEMBERSHIP FOR SELECTED DENOMINATIONS: UNITED STATES, VARIOUS PERIODS[a]

Denomination	Period					
	1920–25	1925–30	1930–35	1930–34	1930–32	1933–35
Roman Catholic	5.1	7.7	2.2	1.2	.2	1.9
Brit.-Amer. Prot.	12.5	(3.5)	(4.0)	(3.0)	1.9	2.2
Major Luth. Bodies	—	9.1	—	7.8	3.1	—
3 Northern Bodies	9.0	1.5	(2.0)	—	.5	.1
3 Southern Bodies	15.4	(4.2)	10.0	—	3.8	4.0
Disciples of Christ	15.9	7.3	4.1	—	1.2	2.7
Cong'l & Christian	9.2	3.6	−1.1	—	−.5	−.9
Prot. Episcopal	8.0	7.2	8.6	—	2.6	5.3
Missouri Synod Luth.	7.2	7.0	14.2	11.5	5.7	5.2
American Luth. Conf.	—	4.2	—	4.9	.7	—
United Lutheran	—	11.3	—	8.1	3.4	—
Ev. Synod of N. A.	—	—	14.5	10.6	3.1	7.0
Southern Baptist	15.9	(5.5)	14.0	—	5.6	5.2
Meth. Episcopal S.	13.8	2.9	5.2	—	1.4	2.6
3 Fundamentalist Groups	—	—	—	—	—	15.8

[a] Figures in parentheses are not quite comparable with the others. Omissions are due in part to incomparable figures, or to the fact that figures were not available or have not been secured. The last three columns were put in to make comparisons not possible in the first three. Minus sign designates decrease in membership. Prepared by Dr. Gilbert K. Robinson.

been greatly reduced during the depression despite the efforts to adjust the cost. The assumption is made by many that the larger the city the greater the decline in membership. This would be an interesting hypothesis for study. They place the decline within the range of 15 per cent to 50 per cent with the modal point at 30 per cent.

During the last decade there have been very great differences in the membership and attendance in Jewish synagogues and temples in large cities, due to population movements within the cities. The Jewish synagogue which has been strategically located in the line of these movements seems not to have felt the effects of the depression in decreased membership even though individual members of such synagogues have suffered. In many smaller places Jewish rabbis testify that there has been little change in attendance and interest because of the depression. In the opinion of these men the German situation and the rising tide of anti-Semitism has had a more profound effect upon American Jewry than has the depression.

THE EVANGELISTIC INDEX AND NET GAINS

There is need for a more accurate index than church membership figures to measure the effects of the depression on church interest. Two such measures are the "net gains" index and the "evangelistic" index.

Many denominations, such as the Presbyterian Church of the U.S.A., and the Congregational churches, list in addition to their total membership figures, the number of those who have been added and lost to the church each year. It is thus possible to get the annual net gain or loss in communicants. Data on the total number of additions each year and the total number of losses through death, letters and revisions are available for the Congregational churches since 1863. From the experience of this church, it would appear that the addition of members decreased, and the loss increased during the last depression so that their greatest loss occurred in 1932.[15]

The "evangelistic" index has been used by Dr. Herman C. Webber[16] in his analysis of Presbyterian church statistics. This index is the ratio of new members each year to the total annual membership. An examination of the membership statistics of this denomination fails to indicate any large fluctuations in the depressions of the 70's or the 90's. The evangelistic index, however, does show variation. The total membership figures and the evangelistic index for the years 1888 to 1921 which are presented in Table II, indicate the greater sensitivity of the latter.

The evangelistic index for the Presbyterian Church in the U.S.A., as worked out by Dr. Webber, indicates great activity from 1826 to 1835, high points in 1843, 1857, 1876, 1894, 1915,

[15] The addition of the statistics of the Christian denomination in 1930 make comparative figures difficult.

[16] Webber, Herman C. *Presbyterian Statistics through One Hundred Years.* Philadelphia: The General Council of the Presbyterian Church in the U.S.A. 1927. Pp. 56ff.

TABLE II
TOTAL MEMBERSHIP AND EVANGELISTIC INDEX, PRESBYTERIAN CHURCH U.S.A.: 1888–1921[a]

Year	Total Membership	Evangelistic Index
1888	706,208	7.0
1889	738,916	7.2
1890	760,530	6.3
1891	790,177	7.3
1892	812,258	6.7
1893	837,088	6.8
1894	877,073	8.3
1895	902,724	7.2
1896	923,515	6.7
1897	939,299	5.8
1898	954,942	5.7
1899	961,334	4.7
1900	983,433	5.5
1901	999,815	5.2
1902	1,024,196	6.2
1903	1,043,547	6.0
1904	1,068,082	5.9
1905	1,090,499	5.6
1906	1,127,267	6.5
1907	1,304,554	5.7
1908	1,275,844	5.6
1909	1,299,165	6.1
1910	1,315,409	5.5
1911	1,330,850	5.2
1912	1,352,876	5.6
1913	1,388,094	6.1
1914	1,427,668	6.2
1915	1,492,619	7.5
1916	1,541,076	6.6
1917	1,579,110	5.9
1918	1,603,628	5.2
1919	1,571,366	3.5
1920	1,602,991	5.8
1921	1,685,859	6.9

[a] Webber, Herman C., *Presbyterian Statistics through One Hundred Years*. The General Council Presbyterian Church in the U. S. A. 1927., P. 45

and 1921. His evangelistic index for ten communions gives the high points as 1832, 1844, 1857, 1866, 1876, 1894, and 1915. All the denominations studied by Dr. Webber followed the same general line. It is not easy to see a consistent correlation between these high points and high or low points in economic activity. It is interesting that Dr. Webber suggests several factors to account for the high and low points but puts very little emphasis upon economic conditions.

It would appear to be worthwhile to study the "net gain" and "evangelistic" indexes over a period of time. Both should be worked out for a number of denominations and an attempt made to correlate them with the business cycle. In such a study various economic indexes might well be used, since the different denominations show regional or urban-rural concentrations.

More difficult to study than quantitative changes in membership, but of perhaps even greater social significance, are possible qualitative changes in church membership. What were the social, economic, political, and personal characteristics of church members who dropped out during the depression, of those who joined the church or came back during the depression? There would be important social implications in changes which resulted in more narrowly restricted church membership—if, for example, families of lower or higher economic status, of a given race or nativity, of a given age or class, etc., left the church. This problem can be attacked only through a study of individual churches and church records. Investigation of this type may be difficult and may be expensive but it is of sufficient importance to warrant the attention of students in this field.

CHURCH ATTENDANCE

Church attendance figures, if they could be secured, would be a further index of the interest of people in churches during depressions in comparison with their interest at other times. It was assumed at the beginning of the depression that church attendance would increase greatly. The general consensus, based on almost the unanimous opinion of clergymen in personal correspondence with the author, seems to be that there has not been a noticeable increase and that where increases did take place these gains were not of long duration.

Brunner and Lorge[17] seek to answer this question for rural regions. Their materials indicate that there has been "a decided falling off on the part of resident members." The middle Atlantic and the South, and the Middle West showed declines. Only the Far West showed increase and that was not on the basis of church membership but of people in the community. The explanation given by Brunner and Lorge is that of "small competing churches, poorly trained ministers and feeble programs."[18] Their attendance summary is given in Table III.

TABLE III
AVERAGE MONTHLY ATTENDANCE IN SELECTED RURAL CHURCHES, ALL DENOMINATIONS, BY REGIONS: 1924, 1930, 1936[a]

Region	Average Monthly Attendance					
	Per Person in Community Population			Per Resident Church Member		
	1924	1930	1936	1924	1930	1936
All regions	1.2	1.1	.96	3.9	3.6	2.8
Middle Atlantic	1.1	1.1	.91	3.5	3.1	2.5
South	1.1	1.0	.95	2.5	3.1	2.4
Middle West	1.6	1.4	.97	5.4	4.0	3.0
Far West	.8	.8	.98	4.5	4.0	3.8

[a] Brunner, Edmund deS. and Lorge, Irving. *Rural Trends in Depression Years.* New York: Columbia University Press. 1937. P. 305

The Sunday morning attendance in 678 Congregational-Christian churches of which there is a complete record for the years 1930-1935, showed that the average attendance rose slightly after the major onset of the depression but possibly not enough to be really significant. (Table IV.)

Attention must be called to the fact that these churches are all within the Congregational-Christian group. The larger number of the churches reporting is in the northeastern section of the United States. Many of the churches are located in the suburbs of the larger cities. These churches are not an adequate

[17] Brunner, Edmund deS., and Lorge, Irving. *Rural Trends in Depression Years.* New York: Columbia University Press. 1937

[18] *Ibid.* P. 305

sample of church attendance in the country as a whole, and it would be highly desirable to have additional studies of this type. There quite probably are a large number of individual churches throughout the country which keep attendance figures, but do not report them to any national headquarters. Perhaps a number of such churches in various denominations can be selected and the depression trends in their average weekly attendance analyzed. If other denominations are found not to vary any more than the Congregationalists, it would suggest that the effects of the depression upon church attendance, although positive, were so small as to be negligible.

TABLE IV
AVERAGE SUNDAY MORNING ATTENDANCE, CONGREGATIONAL-CHRISTIAN CHURCHES: UNITED STATES, 1930–1935[a]

Year	Average Attendance
1930	122.5
1931	124.2
1932	124.8
1933	122.6
1934	120.0
1935	119.5

[a] See Information Series Dec. 12, 1936 Federal Council of the Churches of Christ in America, 105 E. 22nd St., N.Y. See also "Statistical Appendix" Charles J. McCullough in *How to Increase Church Attendance* by Roger W. Babson. New York: Fleming H. Revell Co. 1936.

In studies of church attendance efforts should be made to obtain data on the participation of members in church functions other than the main service. Attendance figures on Lenten services, preaching missions, young people's conferences, church schools, etc., would be valuable supplementation to church service attendance data. Finally, attendance studies should be related to membership trends. Changes in membership would, of course, affect total and average attendance. A study of average attendance per member, together with an attendance frequency distribution, would adequately control this factor.

ADDITIONAL FACTORS TO BE CONSIDERED

Church membership and attendance during the depression may be expected to vary in accordance with a number of factors. The most important perhaps of these are: the previous growth and attendance of the church; its regional, urban-rural or intra-city location; the economic status of the church and its members; the local political situation; the race and nativity of the membership; the general strength and appeal of the denomination; and the leadership abilities of the individual clergyman. All, or as many of these factors as possible, should be considered in a study of this problem. Suggestions for the control of the economic, political, and location factors are indicated elsewhere.[19] In this section some of the items peculiar to the study of church membership and attendance are indicated.

It is frequently contended that denominations grow where they are dominant. Chicago and Illinois studies made by the Department of Research and Survey of the Chicago Theological Seminary and the Chicago Congregational Union show that this appears to have been the case. Those groups which are dominant in any community have a larger proportion of their own natural constituencies than do the groups which are in the minority. Where churches are weak their incoming members do not "find" them. This is especially true of the older, more established denominations whose members have lost the sectarian attitude. On this basis we would expect losses in some areas and gains in others by each of the principal denominations. This is what a study of church population in Illinois revealed so far as Presbyterians are concerned. Other studies should be made in this field. The question to ask would be: Do depressions speed up or retard these concentrations of church membership?

The problem of the relationship of migration[20] to the growth of church membership or to additions to the church may be rather important, especially in local areas. Increases or decreases in the number of persons affiliated with the church or seeking such affiliation result (a) through movement into an area of a particu-

[19] See Chapter V "The Message"; also Appendixes A and B

[20] See Thompson, Warren S. *Research Memorandum on Internal Migration in the Depression* (monograph in this series)

lar church population, (b) by the birth-rate, and (c) by conversion or commitment to church membership.

The population movements of the country are "jelled" in comparison with the rapidity of the western movements during almost the whole of the nineteenth century. There are still rural-urban migrations but these are very much within regions. There is still much variation in birth rates.[21] Some groups are much more vigorous in seeking out new members. Where the population flow ceases and the population movements within a region grow more static, the increases by the birth rate and by conversion are more important. In so far as the effects of the depression may have retarded (or accentuated) migration out of (or into) any particular area, the birth rate and conversion become more (or less) important, in determining the growth of the church or a particular denomination. Once the student has isolated this factor of migration he is in a better position to understand the changes in membership (or additions to membership which he may observe among the churches in a given locality).

Finally, efforts should be made to classify the churches studied according to whether they show increasing, stationary, or declining total membership and attendance; by race and nativity groups; by type of denomination; and by the apparent leadership abilities of individual clergymen. Cross classification of these items should be attempted so far as practicable.

[21] See Thompson, W. S. *Population Problems.* New York: McGraw-Hill Book Co. 1935. Chapter X; Stouffer, S. A. "Trends in the Fertility of Catholics and Non-Catholics." *American Journal of Sociology.* 41:143-166, No. 2. September 1935; Robinson, Gilbert K. "The Catholic Birth-Rate," *American Journal of Sociology.* 41:757-766, No. 6. May 1936; Notestein, Frank W. "Class Differences in Fertility," *Annals of the American Academy of Political and Social Science.* 188: 32-33. November 1936; Jaffe, A. J. "Jewish Birth Rates in the United States." Unpublished MS. See also Stouffer, Samuel A., and Lazarsfeld, Paul F. *Research Memorandum on the Family in the Depression.* (monograph in this series.) Chapter V

Chapter II

Church Finances

THERE were few phases of the national life which were not adversely affected financially during the heart of the depression. One would expect that the religious institutions of the nation, ranging from the local church to the state and national denominational boards and foreign missions boards, would suffer financial losses during this period, and apparently this has been the case.

TOTAL CHURCH CONTRIBUTIONS

In a survey of church finances during the depression, in addition to determining absolute losses, it is important to compare the decline in church receipts and expenditures with decline in expenditures for other items in the national budget, and to observe the shifting emphasis laid upon various types of church expenditures. It is possible to compare the total value of gifts to selected denominations with the national income. This is done in Table V. From these data it can be seen that national income paid out decreased steadily between 1929 and 1933, both in actual dollars and in dollars of the 1929 purchasing power. On the other hand, the amount of money given for congregational expenses, when measured in stable dollars, increased about 13 per cent between 1929 and 1932, and then began declining.

If size of contributions were an adequate index of interest in religion, we should be justified in saying that in the beginning of the depression people became much more interested in the church, but with the onset of recovery their interest markedly declined. However, we do know that church property indebtedness played an important rôle in influencing the amount of the

TABLE V

GIFTS RECEIVED BY SELECTED CHURCHES, FOR CONGREGATIONAL AND NON-CONGREGATIONAL EXPENSES, COMPARED WITH UNITED STATES NATIONAL INCOME PAID OUT: 1929–1935

Year	Total Gifts (in million dollars)[a]	Total Gifts in 1929 Dollars (in millions)[b]	Index (1929 =100)	Gifts for Congregational Expenses (in million dollars)[a]	Gifts for Congregational Expenses in 1929 Dollars (in millions)[b]	Index (1929 =100)	Gifts for Non-Cong'l. Expenses (in million dollars)[a]	Gifts for Non-Cong'l. Expenses in 1929 Dollars (in millions)[b]	Index (1929 =100)	National Income Paid Out (in million dollars)[c]	National Income Paid Out in 1929 dollars (in millions)[b]	Index (1929 =100)
1929	515.0	515.0	100	406.1	406.1	100	108.9	108.9	100	78,632	78,632	100
1930	507.5	539.9	105	401.2	426.8	105	106.3	113.1	104	72,932	77,587	99
1931	475.7	566.3	110	382.1	454.9	112	93.6	111.4	102	61,704	73,457	93
1932	418.6	565.7	110	338.3	457.2	113	80.3	108.5	100	48,362	65,354	83
1933	348.7	484.3	94	284.1	394.6	97	64.6	89.7	82	44,940	62,417	79
1934	299.4	388.8	75	246.2	319.7	79	53.2	69.1	63	50,173	65,160	83
1935	304.7	376.2	73	251.3	310.2	76	53.4	66.0	61	53,587	66,157	84

[a] *Information Service.* March 21 1936. Department of Research and Education. New York: Federal Council of Churches of Christ in America. Data for 25 religious bodies (from United Stewardship Council figures; Harry S. Myers, Sec'y)

[b] Figures in actual dollars deflated by Federal Reserve Bank of New York index of general price level, 1929 = 100

[c] *National Income in the United States, 1929–1935.* Washington, D.C. U. S. Department of Commerce, Bureau of Foreign and Domestic Commerce, 1936

contributions. Large numbers of churches were heavily in debt at the beginning of the depression. As a result the congregations had to make strenuous efforts to meet interest and principal payments. Many special drives and special financial plans were instituted both by denominational leaders and by leaders of local churches. Beginning with 1933, however, bankruptcy proceedings had been so altered that many churches perhaps found it easier to meet their bonded indebtedness. If this were the case, the amount of contributions in the years since 1933 may have declined primarily because of better adjustment of property debts and not because of waning zeal of church members or new financial difficulties.

One way of comparing the drop in church contributions with the drop in the value of consumers' goods—at the same time eliminating the influence of church real estate debts—would be to select those churches within a given denomination (or perhaps within several denominations) which were relatively free from debt at the beginning of the depression and to tabulate the volume of their contributions year by year. The change in the size of these contributions could then be compared with changes in the expenditures in the country as a whole for luxury items, various consumers' items, and income paid out. Data for these last items are available from a number of sources, including the *Biennial Census of Manufactures* and numerous reports from the Department of Commerce.

It would seem from the examination of the data that the church funds "lag" behind the decline in the national income (Table V), but do not come back as quickly as other funds.

From other available data it appears that the contributions of Southern denominations may have turned upward more quickly than those of similar Northern denominations (Figures 2 and 3.) Regional and denominational aspects of this topic should be given thorough study. It is possible that factors other than those operative within the church itself account for variations among regions and denominations. Thus the fact that the Southern Baptists, Methodists, and Presbyterians showed a 7 per cent increase in their contributions received between 1934 and 1935, whereas the similar Northern denominations showed a decrease of 0.2 per cent, might be indicative of an urban-rural or a regional differential rather than of differentiating factors inherent in these denominations. This phenomenon may well reflect regional differentials in "New Deal pump priming." Regional variations are likely to be so important that separate treatment has been devoted to them. (Appendix A.)

It has been suggested frequently in letters to the author that conservative churches fare better in finances in times of depression than do liberal churches. A comparison of certain Lutheran groups with denominations of British-American origin indicates a larger increase in contributions to the former in 1935. The Lutheran groups, generally speaking, are more orthodox than those of British-American origin. If it were certain that no factors other than the type of theology were relevant, these data would tend to bear out the theory stated. It is interesting to note, however, that of the groups with Continental European background the most liberal—the Evangelical and Reformed—may have fared better than the most orthodox—the Missouri Synod Lutheran. Much further study remains to be done. It would be highly desirable to study the church finances of selected churches which are similar so far as possible in all respects but type of theology. Thus, the student should attempt to select churches within the same general area serving approximately the same general types of congregations and having approximately the same general type of financial background at the beginning of the depression. If, after holding all these factors approximately constant, it were found that conservative churches fared better financially than liberal ones, the hypothesis would be established.

CHURCH DEBTS

Separate from any of the considerations, thus far, must be the entire question of church debts—largely building debts ac-

FIGURE 2
CONTRIBUTIONS TO NORTHERN AND SOUTHERN BAPTIST CHURCHES (IN DOLLARS): 1924-1936

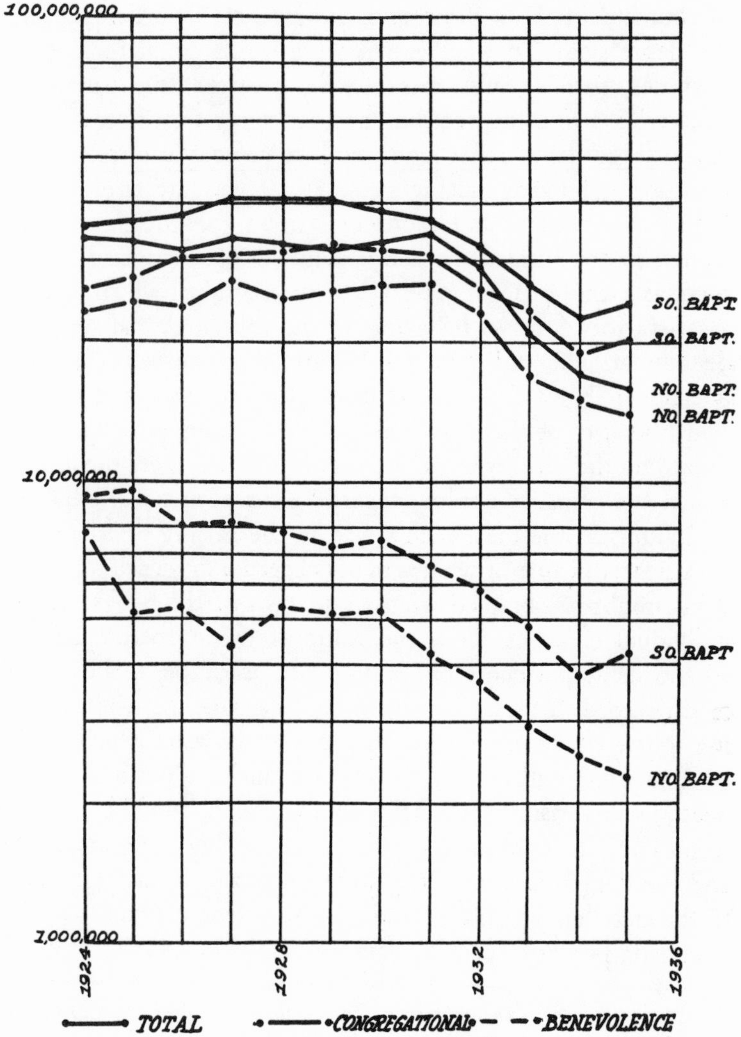

quired during the boom years of 1920-1928. These debts proved to be major financial problems in the depression years. There are many questions which need study. What was the total picture of church debt? How did church groups meet their debts during the depression? To what extent were funds given for specific purposes, such as missionary funds, diverted for current expenses?[1] To what degree did churches agree to, or seek reduction of their debts under legislation which sought to relieve the pressure of bonded indebtedness? What was the effect of the reduction of debts and mortgages upon the prestige of the church in the local community? Did the enactment of "77B" serve as a kind of legal approval of such conduct which made it a satisfactory form of behavior for the church? What were the denominational and regional variations in answers to these questions? How did the credit of the denominations vary? Did liberality of theology make church groups raise questions regarding the validity of high rates of interest? Were the groups which were most scrupulous regarding the payment of debt less scrupulous in the means employed in the raising of funds?

A clearer picture of what actually occurred in regard to church debts might be obtained from an analysis of the books kept in individual churches. Thus the value of the property, the size of the debt, payments on debt, revisions of debt, should all be on record in these accounts. Data may also be available on the source of income during the depression years which might be compared with source of income during "normal" years. Special plans arising, such as the Goodwin plan,[2] might be studied in an effort to determine extent to which they were employed and the degree in which they were successful in raising funds. If the detailed financial records of sufficient churches can be obtained, perhaps specific types of churches can be selected

[1] That such practices were sometimes found is indicated in personal correspondence of the author with clergymen and church officials.

[2] This plan has often been referred to in *The Christian Century*

FIGURE 3

CONTRIBUTIONS TO METHODIST EPISCOPAL CHURCH AND METHODIST EPISCOPAL CHURCH SOUTH (IN DOLLARS):

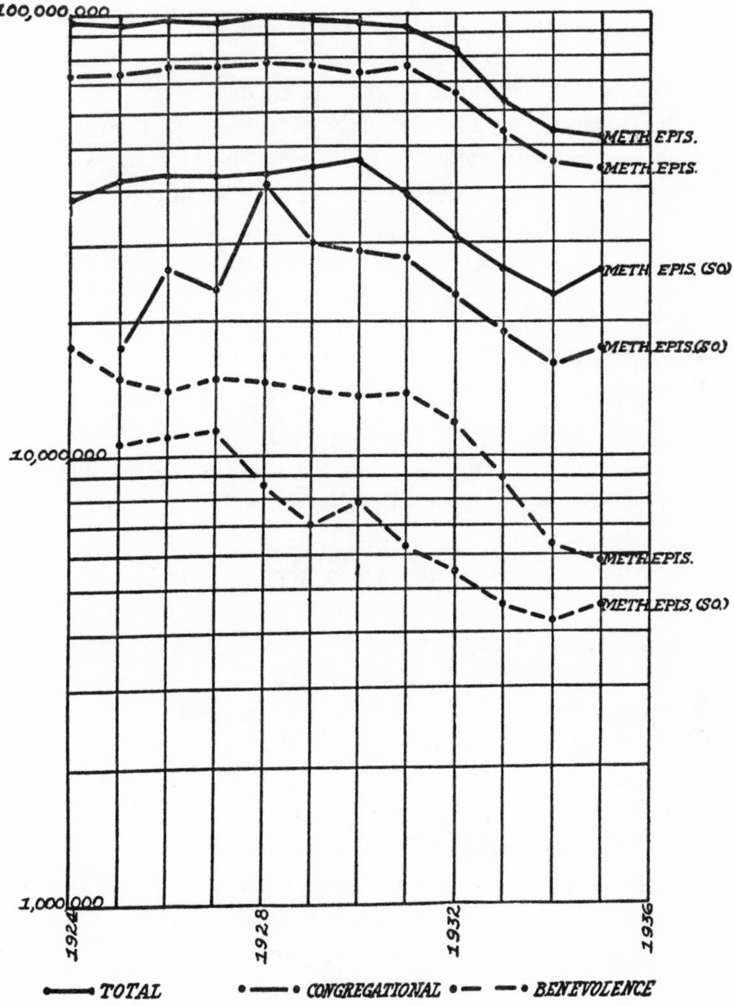

for comparative purposes, as conservative and liberal, urban and rural, etc.

It has been suggested that most churches found it very easy to borrow heavily during prosperous times.[3] If this was the case, an analysis of financial records might reveal information on this matter. The ratio of the size of mortgages to the value of the property should be a fairly good index of credit. Where credit is not easily obtained, the size of the mortgages in comparison to the total value of the property should be the smallest. If churches can be compared with residential and business property in this respect, some evaluation of the churches' financial policy and position may be possible.

CHANGES IN SOURCES OF INCOME

Where did the decreases or increases in church income occur? Where were decreases in contributions first evident? Where were the percentages of decrease the greatest? What happened to church endowments during the depression? Were church investments well made? Who sacrificed the most for the church—the rich or the poor? Many clergymen[4] report a more even distribution of the financial burdens of the church during the depression, and an increased democratization in church membership.

If a frequency distribution showing the number of contributions by size of contribution can be obtained for a group of selected local churches over a period of years, many of those questions can be answered. For example, if it were found that in 1929, 50 per cent of the contributions were made by 25 per cent of the contributors, whereas in 1933 the upper 25 per cent contributed 75 per cent of the total funds, we should conclude that a small group tended to maintain the church through the depression. If the reverse were true, the upper 25 per cent contributing only 25 per cent of all the money, it would indicate a

[3] Holt, Ivan Lee. *Search for a New Strategy in Protestanism.* Nashville: Copesbury Press. 1936. Chapters I and II

[4] Based on personal correspondence

democratization of church finances during the depression.

In an attempt to answer the question as to where contributions were cut first, the following procedure may be useful. Studies might be made of the contributions of total or sample contributors to selected churches during the boom and the depression years, and changes in the sizes of their contributions noted. It may be possible to set up a table showing the number of contributors by size of contribution during the prosperous years, and to follow the members of each class interval through the depression years. The average size of contribution can be calculated for each year for each class interval and percentage changes noted. Thus, it might be found that those who had contributed the most in prosperous years showed the greatest decline. The problems raised by persons dying and/or leaving the church must be considered. If the turnover in contributing church members has been too great the value of this type of analysis would be restricted.

Theoretically, all other things being equal, the relative proportion of the family's budget which is spent on the church might be regarded as an index of its interest in that institution. If, then, during the depression, it became more interested in the church, we should find the family contributing a larger proportion of its budget to the church than during prosperous times. Differentials in the rigidity of the price structure, in the elasticity of demand for various commodities, and in the character of the expenditures of families on different budget levels, complicate this type of study.

It may be worth while, however, to analyze family expenditure budgets of comparable groups before and during the depression in an attempt to measure the relationship of expenditures for religious affairs to expenditures for other consumer's items. Did families on different budgetary levels tend to appropriate a continuously larger or smaller share toward the church as they lost income during the advent of the depression? In this connection it is interesting to observe that in a study of families in Washington, D.C., Ogburn found that the percentage of the total income allocated for religious purposes increased as the family's wealth increased and decreased as its size increased.[5]

When we use the size of the total contributions, or the per capita contribution, as an index of church interest we must keep several considerations in mind. First of all, if we use such indexes for different regions of the country, the financial status of the various regions must be considered. We would need a general financial index for the particular regions with which we are dealing. The per capita contribution, for example, of the Southern Baptists, is sometimes compared with the per capita contribution of other groups in the United States without any reference to the respective financial status of the groups considered. Even comparison of church finances within the same region must be carefully considered, because of fluctuations, over a period of time, in purchasing power within the region. In using the per capita contribution as an index of church interest one must also be on guard for unusually large gifts from individuals, special drives, or other special circumstances.

CHURCH EXPENDITURES

Studies should also be conducted on the effects of the depression on absolute and proportionate church expenditures. A description of church expenditures would illuminate not only its financial problems but also the changing character of its program and activities.[6] Research on this problem must adapt itself to the record keeping systems of the various denominations. In general, however, it would be well to follow this outline:

I. *Home Expenses*
   (1) Ministerial support (may be broken up in groups)
   (2) Pensions and annuities

---

[5] Ogburn, William F. "Analysis of the Standard of Living in the District of Columbia in 1916." *Journal of the American Statistical Association.* June 1919

[6] See Chapter VI "Program and Activities" for further treatment of this problem

(3) Other local church expenses
  A. Other salaries
  B. Church school expenses
  C. Building maintenance (heat, light, etc.)
  D. Others
(4) Property debts and improvements

II. *Outside Expenses*
(1) Foreign Missions
(2) Home Missions; "Other beneficences"
(3) Education
(4) Social work rendered away from church
  A. Orphanages
  B. Home for the aged
  C. Hospitals

So far as church records permit, time series should be constructed of absolute and proportionate expenditures for each item in the categories listed. In such time comparisons the data should be reported in stable dollars.

If the percentage distribution of the expenditures each year is calculated, shifts in expenditures will be particularly discernible. Thus, for example, it might be found that in the early years of the depression bonded indebtedness accounted for a larger portion of each dollar expended than was the case in prosperous years. A preliminary investigation for a few denominations shows that the greatest decrease in expenditures is found in contributions for new buildings and improvements. The next greatest decreases occur in the payment of debts (largely building debts) and, in appropriations, for benevolences. Local church expenditures, which include the pastor's salary, decrease least. Sample data on expenditures for congregational matters and for benevolences are given in Table VI.

In general, contributions for benevolences decreased more sharply than those for congregational expenses. The Protestant Episcopal church was the one major exception to this general rule in the 1930's.

Various suggestions have been advanced in regard to what has been happening in the re-allocation of church expenditures during the depression.[7] It has been suggested, for example, that during these times, churches, by virtue of the necessity of self-preservation, have not only ceased to give liberally for missionary work but have also lost interest in such work. Moreover, it has also been suggested that churches have even neglected the larger community in which they lived, that they have become institu-

TABLE VI
PERCENTAGE CHANGES IN CONTRIBUTIONS TO CONGREGATIONAL EXPENSES AND TO BENEVOLENCES, FOUR DENOMINATIONS[a]

Denomination	Years	Percentage Changes in Contributions to	
		Cong'l. Exp.	Benev.
Methodist Episcopal	1930–1935	−39[b]	−51
Presbyterian U. S.	1928–1934	−40	−58
Presbyterian U. S. A.	1929–1934	−44	−55
Congregational	1928–1934	−42	−55

[a] Denominational yearbooks
[b] Includes salaries of district superintendents and bishops

tional minded and have grown "introverted." These ideas might be verified or refuted by studying the extent to which churches eliminated expenditures other than those required for immediate needs, i.e., pastors' salaries, heating, lighting, etc.

Did the churches shift their funds from social service work, old peoples' homes, orphanages, hospitals, neighborhood house programs and similar activities, into kinds of work or church institutions which might be more productive of new members? The possible extent of these changes in policy might be ascertainable from a study of proportionate expenditures.[8] That the allocation of the church dollar directly expresses the will of the members of the church does not always seem to be the case. For example, there has been considerable agitation on the part

[7] By clergy and interested lay people in personal correspondence

[8] See the section on institutional churches and neighborhood houses in Chapter VI, "Program and Activities." Doubtless the recent social security legislation will speed up changes in church money contributed and expended for old peoples' homes.

of some individuals to have proportionate expenditures for home and foreign missions changed during the period of the depression. In some cases radical changes have been made; in others, however, little or no change occurred. Many of the church boards are so organized that changes occur only through long and tedious processes. Very often the opinion of the congregation has to register slowly. It is possible that congregation opinion regarding depression policies may not be reflected in church activities during the depression. Officials are usually influential in determining the character of expenditures, particularly those not directly concerned with the needs of the local church.

Each of the items in the outline which has been presented for the study of church expenditures might be further subdivided into more specific problems. A number of questions might be asked, for example, in regard to the effect of the depression on staff salaries in individual churches. What staff members were dispensed with first? What reductions were effected in the salaries of the various staff members? Were salaries reduced on a graduated basis? To what extent were other members of the staff protected by the minister? What was the effect on the congregation and the community of such effort on the part of the minister? Questions of this character should be raised about each category in the outline and answered as thoroughly as church records and other data permit.

The study of church finances during the depression involves not only the program of denominational policy and large lump expenditure, but the experience of the local church as well. It was frequently necessary for regional or national organizations to help local churches whose communities could not support them. The Chicago Congregational Union, for example, made vigorous effort in this direction. Its staff sought to secure facts on what was happening to churches because of reduced incomes and presented these facts to each of four conferences of churches.[9] An effort should be made to describe the extent and

[9] For further materials on Protestant finances before the depression see Fahs,

character of local church dependence on regional or national organizations.

The foregoing discussion has centered mainly on the finances of Protestant groups. Similar analyses should also be attempted for the Jewish and Roman Catholic groups. Since no denominational data are available for the Jewish group as a whole, studies of this religious body would have to depend on the data available in individual synagogues. Similarly, so far as the author knows, there are no general summary figures on Roman Catholic finances. Efforts should be made to secure such data from the bishops. From conversation with priests and lay members of the Catholic church, it seems that there were a number of Roman Catholic churches which experienced financial difficulties. The membership in the Roman Catholic church in the United States has been greatly influenced by immigration in recent years. Many of these immigrant peoples are of the poorer classes. As a result, separate parishes frequently have not been able to meet the needs of their indigent members. A dependence of the poor parishes upon those of greater wealth has, in some instances, been necessary. This is indicated in a document by Dr. E. C. Hughes on the relief situation in the Canadian Catholic church. The Canadian experience, although very different from that in the United States, reveals the changes which have taken place due to the depression.[10] The Roman Catholic church, as was the practice of many other churches, borrowed, and built heavily during the twenties, and consequently was burdened with debt during the thirties. "There are many Roman Catholic organizations which will find it exceedingly difficult to pay their debts unless radical reductions take place," is the statement by a well-informed Catholic priest.[11]

Charles H. *Trends in Protestant Giving*. New York: Institute of Social and Religious Research. 1929

[10] See Appendix C.

[11] Based on personal conferences

Chapter III

The Clergy

IT SEEMS clear from the studies of church finances that the current expenses of the church were cut less than the benevolences. Many churches had debts which cut heavily into the current expenses and into the minister's salary. There were many discussions of financial affairs and sometimes tensions between ministers and people on the topic. In many cases of large churches there was reduction of staff. The duties of ministers during the depression were enlarged, in terms of administration, religious education, supervision of group meetings, the raising of funds, caring for needy cases, and counselling. Some ministers felt thwarted in their plans. Much more care needed to be exercised regarding their utterances. The minister was in the focus of many problems and much confusion. Reports from state secretaries and officials as well as ministers reveal attitudes of worry, frustration, and defeat on the part of many ministers during the depression.

In an attempt to evaluate the effects of the depression on the church it is of importance to study any changes which may have occurred among the clergy. It can reasonably be expected that changes in the number of clergymen, in their salaries, opportunities for advancement, provisions for retirement, and changes in their duties might vitally affect the function of the church. Of even greater importance in this respect, although more difficult to study, are possible changes in the attitudes of the clergy toward the political and economic order, toward the church, toward religion, toward their congregations, and in their conceptions of their own rôles. Suggestions for the investigation of these problems are outlined below.

NUMBER OF CLERGYMEN

1. Number of Ministers

Changes in the number of ministers serving are probably more a function of a long-time trend than of cyclical business variations. This statement can easily be tested by plotting the number of "effective ministers"[1] over a period of years. The fitting of an appropriate curve to a time series can be used in an analysis. If there has been a drop during the depression years, the deviations from the fitted line should be larger and more negative here than in prosperous years.

Another question that may, perhaps, be raised here is whether or not the number of churches having no ministers fluctuated with the business cycle. Theoretically, the number of ministers could remain constant through a depression and yet a number of small churches which never had ministers could close down. The result would imply a contraction of the potential market for the services of ministers.

2. Number of "Local Preachers"

These are persons who have received licenses to preach, but are not effective ministers. In some instances, they represent persons just entering church work, although in other cases, they represent "old-timers" who have served in this capacity for a number of years and have never advanced. Their total number, year by year, should be analyzed in the same manner as that suggested for the analysis of the ministers.

It is theoretically possible that the number of local preachers may have increased during the depression. If this were the case,

[1] The terms used here and in the next five sections apply to the Methodist Episcopal Church. Various denominations have some of the same types of data available, although different designations are used.

either one or both of the following interpretations is possible: first, that many local preachers who would have risen out of that class and become effective ministers failed to do so during the depression; second, that many churches in an effort to decrease expenditures may have substituted local preachers for ministers. This latter possibility could be tested by schedules for individual churches to see whether or not there had been a change from ministers to preachers during the depression.

3. Number of Ministers Admitted to Full Membership

This category represents the demand for new ministers. If the demand decreased during the depression, either through the closing of churches, the inability of congregations to support ministers or the substitution of local preachers for ministers, then the number of new ministers admitted should have declined. This would not necessarily be the case in a freely competitive profession such as law, where all who master certain minimum requirements are admitted to the bar. The ministry, however, represents a closed universe to which additions are made only when needed. The number of ministers admitted to full membership can be analyzed in much the same manner as was suggested for the effective ministers and the local preachers, and it may be expected that it will be a more sensitive index of depression effects than the total number of ministers or preachers. A good device for comparative studies would be the construction of time series showing the ratio of new ministers admitted in a given year to the total ministers.

4. Number of Ministers Received on Trial

This category may be the most sensitive index of the need for additions to the ministry. Whereas the category "number of ministers admitted to full membership" may be a function, to a certain extent, of forces operating in the past, the number of ministers received on trial represents, for the most part, individuals just entering the profession. If there has been a large drop in demand for new ministers during the depression, it should presumably be evident in a decrease in the number of ministers received on trial. Indexes similar to those described above should be constructed.

5. Number of Ministers Supernumerary and Retired

To a large extent, this represents the old men who are no longer able to perform and as such is a function of the biological process. However, since there is no reason for the number of old persons to fluctuate with the business cycle, any such fluctuations observable in the number of supernumerary and retired ministers may reflect depression policy and practice on retirement. For example, if the number of ministers who retire during the depression is much smaller than during prosperity, it may reflect a desire on the part of the old ministers to remain in service or greater leniency on the part of congregations. Comparative studies should be attempted through construction of a time series for various groupings of churches showing the relation of ministers annually retired to total ministers.

6. Number of Ministers Who Died, Located, Withdrew and Were Expelled

The number of ministers who died is also largely a function of the biological process and as such should show no great cyclical variations. The others comprise a very small number of ministers who have dropped out for one reason or another. The main reason for including this category is to complete the picture of the numerical size of the ministry.

All of the above data can be set in a table (for each conference, denomination or combination of denominations) as in Table VII, for example.

In analyzing this data, the various denominations and church groupings by such factors as regional, urban-rural, or intra-

TABLE VII
MOVEMENT OF MINISTERS, DENOMINATION Y, BY YEARS

Year	Number of Ministers Effective	Number Admitted to Full Membership	Ratio of Number Admitted to Number Effective	Number Received on Trial	Ratio of Number Received on Trial to Number Effective

Year	Number Supernumerary and Retired	Ratio of Number Retired to Number Effective	Number Local Preachers	Ratio of Number of Preachers to Number Effective	Number Separated, Other Reasons	Ratio of Number Separated to Number Effective

city location, economic status, etc., could be compared by means of the ratios indicated. In studies of other denominations or in comparative studies it will of course be necessary to adapt the categories employed to the differences in organization which occur. Moreover the data reported vary greatly in their reliability. In general it is felt that profitable studies of the type suggested can be made. However, investigators should be careful to evaluate the reliability of their statistics with which they work.

VERTICAL AND HORIZONTAL MOBILITY

Studies should also be attempted of the effects of the depression on processes of horizontal and vertical mobility, that is, on the transfers of clergymen from their own churches to churches on the same, higher, or lower levels. It has been suggested that pastors were "frozen" in their places and that men with good positions held on to them.[2] Data for answering these questions are available in the various yearbooks, conference reports, and other published volumes. In the yearbook of the Presbyterian Church in the U. S., for example, the name, church, and salary of every minister in the denomination is listed.

If, on the basis of the salary paid the minister, three or four classes of churches are defined, it is easily determined whether from year to year a given clergyman has moved horizontally (in the same salary level) or vertically (to a higher or lower salary level). By following individuals through from one year to the next, it is thus possible to determine how many ministers have moved horizontally and how many vertically during any given year. It is also possible to divide vertical mobility into movements upward and downward, respectively. Each of these figures can then be expressed as a percentage of the total number of ministers as of that year. Depression influences can be determined by plotting these percentages in a time series. Ministers who drop out of service from one year to the next, through death, retirement, or a change in occupation can be studied in a similar manner to insure that such separations do not seriously disturb mobility studies.

Vertical mobility also may be measured in another manner. The investigator could trace the church connections of sample groups of ministers who were ordained or admitted as ministers during the ten year periods 1905 to 1914, and 1915 to 1924, respectively. Ministers usually begin in the lowest salary classes. It is possible to determine what percentage of those of the 1905 to 1914 group advanced to higher salary levels during the first ten years of their work, and to compare these percentages with similar data for the 1915 to 1924 group. If the depression has slowed down vertical mobility, then a smaller proportion of the

[2] Based on personal correspondence

latter group should reach higher levels than of the former group. In an analysis of this nature, a number of factors such as education, denomination, region, etc., should be taken into account. The samples of ministers in each group studied should be matched as closely as possible.

SEMINARY GRADUATES[3]

Were there more or fewer seminary students and graduates during depression years than prosperous years? Was there any selection involved in students who entered or dropped from seminaries during the depression? How many graduates were placed and what kind of placements were they given? How did placements during the depression compare with placements in predepression years? Data on the number of students in and graduates from Methodist Episcopal schools of theology are available in the yearbooks of the organization. The Presbyterian Church of the U. S. presents more detailed data in regard to both students and graduates in their yearbooks. Neither denomination, however, presents data on placements of graduates. Such data would have to be obtained directly from the students or the schools.

SALARIES

To what extent were the salaries of ministers decreased during the depression? In general it is known that salaries were sharply curtailed but a study of this problem would throw more direct light on the personal hardships of clergymen in the general economic slump. Another problem of some importance in this regard is that concerning differentials in the salary decreases effected. It is the opinion of a number of qualified observers that clergymen with medium and small salaries suffered

[3] For ways in which theological students have been studied see *The Education of American Ministers*. New York: Institute of Social and Religious Research. 1934. 4 vols.; see especially May, Mark A., *et al.* Vol. III. "The Institutions That Train Ministers."

larger percentage decreases than did those with larger salaries.[4] This opinion can easily be tested.

Other questions concerning the salaries of ministers during the depression which should be studied are: Did the range in salaries increase or decrease? Did the proportion of the salaries paid indirectly increase? Did the proportion of the salaries paid in cash decrease? What per cent of the salaries promised by the congregations were actually paid?

One factor that should be taken into consideration in studies of this type is the possible hidden drop in salaries that may have occurred. For example, a minister who wished to retain his salary status might make arrangements to contribute to the church the amount which his congregation wished to deduct from his salary. Thus a minister with a salary of $2,500 might continue to receive that amount in salary but would, by arrangement, contribute $500 to the church so that his actual salary was only $2,000. Such a hidden cut in his salary would not appear in the yearbook records. Finally, in connection with the problems of salaries, it would be worthwhile to investigate the question as to whether, during the depression, weak churches tended to be invaded by inferior preachers, who maintained that it was not right for the minister to make a fixed charge and that they were willing to begin with "just what the people could pay."

DUTIES OF MINISTERS

Was there any shift in the duties of ministers during the depression? It has been suggested[5] that the enforced departure of directors of religious education from many churches materially increased the duties of many pastors. The number of churches with directors of religious education has never been great, but the largest churches with the largest congregations have had them. The whole question of the greater use of volunteers as

[4] Personal correspondence with clergymen

[5] Personal correspondence from clergymen and interested lay persons

against the paid employee of the church has also been brought to the fore by the depression. This was one of the specific ways in which a number of churches sought to reduce their budgets. Very often hardships were thrust upon staff members who were compelled to look elsewhere for employment. The general trend seems to have been in the direction of reducing professional help and of increasing the burden of church administration.[6]

Greater burdens were therefore usually borne by the minister, because it has been universally assumed that he is the one indispensable staff member of the church. In a number of cases the director of religious education had been an effective "vice-president" of the church. When he retired, in addition to other added duties, the minister was also compelled to assume the task of directing volunteers.

The presence of actual crises in the homes of church members created new demands of counselling to which many ministers responded. Ministers perhaps came into closer touch with family life during the depression. Many ministers[7] feel that they were brought closer to their people. Some regret that this reduced their time for reading and study. Before public relief was furnished on a large scale indigent cases occupied the attention and interest of many ministers.

These are but a few of the more important ways in which the duties of the minister may have been changed by depression problems. A study of these changes would necessitate the use of schedules or personal interview. It is likely, however, that ministers and other staff members could answer questions concerning their duties during the depression with a high degree of reliability.

CHANGES IN ATTITUDES[8]

The studies which are outlined above are mainly quantitative in character and would throw considerable direct light and

[6, 7] Personal correspondence

[8] See also Chapter V

permit many inferences on problems of the clergy during the depression. Perhaps the greatest interest in the effects of the depression on the clergy, however, centers around such matters as possible changes in their attitudes toward:

1. The social, political, and economic order
2. The church
3. Religion
4. Their congregations
5. Their conceptions of their own rôles

Research into these problems is necessarily more difficult, must essentially be based on questionnaires, rating scales, case studies and life history materials, and will probably be inconclusive. Such research, however fragmentary it may be, would at least illuminate what are now unknown phenomena.

During the course of the last few years the attitudes of a large portion of the American public toward economic, political, and social institutions seem to have changed considerably. It seems reasonable to expect that the clergy has not been exempted from the influences which have caused such changes. It is clear that modifications in the attitudes of the clergy on these matters may vitally affect the rôle and the influence of the church.

A number of hypotheses might well be posited for the study of this problem. Among these might be:

(1) *The attitudes of the clergy as a group became more liberal on economic, political, and social issues during the depression.*[9]

(2) *The attitudes of the clergy toward political, economic, and social problems changed in the direction of that of their congregations.*

(3) *The attitudes of the clergy toward political, economic, and social problems changed in the direction of that of their boards of trustees.*

---

[9] One must always keep in mind the difficulty of securing a generalization on a large heterogeneous grouping.

Did the depression change the attitudes of the clergy toward the church as a social institution, toward religion, toward their congregations? In view of the tremendous pressure on the church and on the clergy occasioned by the economic slump, it seems safe to observe that these attitudes have been affected. An important question, but difficult to study, is that of the permanency of the changed attitudes. When good times return do ministers swing back somewhere near their former positions or do permanent changes occur?

It would be interesting to know the conceptions of the clergy of the rôle of the church as an institution in dealing with depression problems. What did they conceive to be the function of the church during this trying period? What was their conception of their own rôles? Among the hypotheses on this matter which might be studied are the following:

(1) *The intense and widespread unemployment and poverty occasioned by the depression led the clergy to adopt the belief that the church should permanently abandon in favor of government relief all efforts to provide charity or relief for its distressed members.*

(2) *The problems created by the depression led the clergy to believe that the church should provide a personal rather than a social message to its members.*

(3) *The depression accelerated the secularization of the attitudes of the clergy.*

(4) *The depression led the clergy to regard themselves as leaders of social, political, and economic reform.*

(5) *The depression brought many ministers a sense of defeat in accomplishing the good life for their members.*

Doubtless many ministers have suffered a sense of defeat during the depression. This has been true of ministers in all denominations. State secretaries report that in the depth of the depression ministers would write in saying, "What is the matter with me? I do not seem to be able to get anywhere." Lynd says: "The ministers are themselves harried, overworked, perplexed that religion has not vindicated itself more in the depression."[10] The difficulties of specific parishes are often responsible for these attitudes but the defeatism was widespread.[11]

The questionnaire, the rating scale, and the case study, are the only means through which the questions raised above can be answered. There is room for exercising ingenuity in devising satisfactory instruments for the study of these problems. It may be worthwhile experimenting with the possibilities of questionnaires and rating scales in which the persons are asked to indicate predepression and depression attitudes as they recall them. The results should be enlightening even if they reveal only what the persons think has happened to their attitudes.

To illustrate, the following inquiries might be incorporated into a questionnaire. (This list of items is presented merely to illustrate an approach which may prove profitable in studies of attitude phenomena.)

YOUR ATTITUDE

	Before the Depression			During the Depression		
	Extensively	Some	Not at all	Extensively	Some	Not at all
1. Should the church support the child labor amendment?						
2. Should the church emphasize individual salvation?						
3. Should the church emphasize spiritual aid to its members?						
4. Should the church support organized labor in collective bargaining?						
5. Should the church support demands for the more equitable distribution of wealth?						

[10] Lynd, Robert S. and Helen M. *Middletown in Transition.* New York: Harcourt, Brace & Co. 1937. P. 308

[11] Clare, Tom. "Some Effects of the Depression upon the Personality of the Pastor." *Theological Magazine of the Evangelical Synod of North America.* 61:170-175, No. 3. May 1 1933

FACTORS TO BE CONTROLLED AND LIMITATIONS OF SOURCES OF DATA

All of the factors mentioned above may be studied by:

(1) denomination
(2) conference (diocese, synod, etc.)
(3) education and training of clergymen
(4) age of clergymen
(5) experience of clergymen
(6) urban and rural areas
(7) city size
(8) geographical, social, and/or economic regions

The consideration of these variables in any study might disclose, for example, that the more poorly trained ministers suffered larger salary cuts, or that younger men fared better than older men. In so far as data are available, all of these variables should be considered, because the results obtained through ignoring these factors might reflect group rather than depression differences.

The statistical data available for purposes of analysis, although rather voluminous, are not the best desirable.[12] To begin with, not all individual churches send in complete figures each year, yet the totals as reported in the yearbooks do not adequately indicate this fact. Another error observable in the Methodist data is that some churches lag a year in their statistical reports. The result is that the totals in the annual volumes often include data for some churches for the preceding year. The investigator is therefore confronted with the necessity of either obtaining the missing data so as to complete the denominational (or conference) reports for each year, or of selecting a list of churches which supply adequate returns each year and following these churches through a series of years. The latter method is dangerous because for certain purposes complete coverage is needed. If we try to study the effects of the depression on the total number of ministers, it is possible that

[12] See, for a criticism of church statistics, *Methodist Yearbook*. New York: Methodist Book Concern. 1932. Section XII. Pp. 322-324

those churches which are irregular in submitting their reports tend more than the others to discharge ministers during depression periods. If sample churches are selected it is important, therefore, that they adequately represent the group studied. Finally, another source of error that must be carefully watched arises from the fact that the fiscal year of the reporting churches is not always the same. Regional or denominational fiscal totals based on variant fiscal periods may result in serious distortions of the data.

Despite these limitations of the source data it is the opinion of the writer that most of the questions raised in this chapter can be answered satisfactorily. Investigators, however, will find it necessary to be cautious and critical in their use of published church statistics.

Chapter IV

Secularization: General Considerations

EFFECTS of the depression on the message of the church will be discussed in Chapter V. Effects of the depression on the program and activities of the church will be discussed in Chapter VI. In these two chapters there will be recurrent attention to what has been called the process of secularization of religious attitudes and activities during the depression. This subject must occupy a central place in any discussion of the effects of the depression on religion. Because of its great importance, it seems desirable to devote a few introductory pages to the concept of secularization, viewed not alone in the light of the depression but also more generally.

The earlier meaning of the term "secularization" was the removal of some function from ecclesiastical control to some control outside the church. The "seculum" referred to the age in which one lived. The secular order was the temporal order, the "this world" order; the religious had to do with the eternal. God was identified with the eternal. By analogy, the secular came to refer to the worldly as against the religious or the sacred, to which God is related. Secularization rigidly defined, then, would be the process by which a function is removed from the control of a religious institution, with a philosophy that God controls, to the larger community, or some institution which does not recognize the religious motivation. Strictly speaking, the term does not mean that the function as such is performed in a better or worse fashion. "I shall use the term 'secularism,'" says John Bennett, "for that characteristic of our world according to which life is organized apart from God as though God did not exist. . . . From a religious point of view it means that the highest objects of devotion are human ideals and human causes which emerge in the social process."[1] It must be pointed out that not all phases of secularism take on an anti-religious attitude. Secularization as a process does not imply a positive propaganda against religion. It is probably true that in Europe the anti-church nature of secularism is much more pronounced than it is in America.

The discussions regarding secularization in modern church groups indicate that there is a consciousness of the chasm which exists between the church and the remainder of society. The process of secularization is not found where there is complete identification of church and state but only where the church is set off against the remainder of society. Any set of conditions which increases the consciousness of the church that it is set off from the rest of the world makes possible conditions in which secularization may take place. The church is in a dilemma; if it identifies itself completely with the social order it loses a certain objectivity in criticism; if it sets itself off it is always in danger of losing that which it conceives its province to be.

Secularization, in the wider usage of the term, may be thought of as occurring in either of two main ways.

First, there is the process by which activities once performed by the church (government, education, philanthropy, etc.) have been taken over by the larger community, as the state, and have come to be considered as falling outside the domain of the church and as having no need of religion for their maintenance. It is not necessarily secularization when functions hitherto confined to the church are transferred to other organizations, if those organizations simply become the instruments of the church for maintaining the ideals and convictions created first within the church. Some religions seek to leaven all institutions. Education

[1] *Christianity and Our World.* New York: Association Press. 1936. P. 1

does not become secular because it comes under the state but because it ceases to have a religious frame of reference. Education, for the most part, did go through the process of secularization here in America when it came under the state. Religious groups that have no interest in "education" may help in a negative fashion to push on the secularization of education. The community itself comes to think of them as non-religious.

Second, there is also the process by which the church reaches out into the community to find activities such as recreation and community service which churches have not recognized as a part of their "sacred order" and to include these so-called secular activities along with those which have been definitely religious. It is secularization when the church, incorporating these activities, recognizes them as unrelated to the essentials of the doctrines and beliefs of the church and does not relate these activities to the main purposes of the church.

A form of secularization is found, also, when the churches come to judge themselves by secular standards such as are found in the booster psychology as "bigger and better." That some churches have beaten a retreat from this position during the depression is suggested by the writer's correspondence with ministers and laymen.

When an activity which was once performed by the church is taken over by the community or state, the church is not secularized by that process. When the churches give up a function like ordinary education in the three R's the process, and not the church, is secularized. The activities which churches perform may, however, be limited. This has been true of so many activities that the question is now asked: "Are there any important functions remaining for the church?" It is at this point that questions are raised regarding the irrelevant nature of churches today. Other organizations and groups are working on the larger questions of the meaning and purposes of life, i.e., on salvation in the broader usage of the term. Some writers give the answer that although others deal with the purposes of life, the churches have distinctive answers to these questions.

With the increased interpenetration of various cultural elements has come a more complete integration and unification of all the phases of life. A vital question is whether or not the church may still exercise control by means of a message which must have a bearing on all of life and deal with problems which have become the work of specialists in a new compartmentalization of life.

A FRAME OF REFERENCE IN WHICH TO STUDY SECULARIZATION

1. General Considerations

(1) Secularization must be thought of in terms of the messages and teachings of the church and also in terms of the practices and programs of the church. It is unsound to attempt to come to conclusions on such a topic without a broad study of the interrelated phases of a church's life.

(2) It must be recognized that secularization of the activities of churches has had a long history and that, in the history of the church, which is a long-lived institution, the depression constitutes a very short period.

(3) The secularization of the activities of churches at one period in the history of the world has been in terms of one content while at another period it has been in the terms of another content, although at times several phases of the church's life have been linked together; for example, the separation of church and state has involved the separation of much of the work of education from the church.

(4) The factors and forces which have been responsible for the secularization of church activities are varied from period to period although the developments of science and scientific attitudes seem to have been dominant factors in much of this process.

(5) While the process of secularization has been going on for centuries and while G. J. Holyoake wrote his *Principles of Secularism* as early as 1885, the discussion of secularism as a foe of the church has taken on added vigor since the Jerusalem meeting of the International Missionary Council in 1928 in which Dr. Rufus M. Jones[2] clearly outlined the history of the forces making for secularization and the problems which face the church as a result of this movement. The recent movements of Communism and Fascism in which the totalitarian state plays a dominant rôle have greatly increased the discussion of the topic.[3]

(6) If we think of secularization as a longtime trend we must also think of the counter movements of thought, sometimes definite social movements which have slowed down or retarded the trend. Religious groups seem to have a way of rising with vigor and passing through various stages of development. One must note these rising currents of religious life as they inhibit the general trend toward secularization. Note the rise of the religions of the disinherited.[4]

(7) In formulating specific questions we might seek to see the things which speed up or slow down the trend. A catalogue of the aspects of the depression which we would expect to speed up and slow down secularization, respectively, follows:

2. Some Factors Which May Have Speeded Up Secularization in the Depression

(1) The reduction of funds on the part of churches has compelled many of them to relinquish activities which have not been central to their organization and thus has secularized the

[2] New York: International Missionary Council. 1928. Vol. I. Chapter VII

[3] Pauck, Wilhelm. "The Crisis of Religion." Niebuhr, H. Richard, Pauck, Wilhelm, and Miller, Francis P. *The Church against the World*. Chicago: Willett Clark and Co. 1935

[4] Niebuhr, H. Richard. *The Social Sources of Denominationalism*. New York: Henry Holt and Co. 1929

activities which churches have performed. This has meant greater emphasis upon those phases of the church's life which have dealt more specifically with religious teachings. The church itself, therefore, has not been secularized by this process but the activities which it once performed are secularized.

(2) While church funds have been reduced, government agencies have felt called upon to use the unemployed in various ways. These agencies have supplied workers for the very activities in which churches themselves have engaged—clubs, classes, forums, recreational activities, and counselling.[5] Some might argue that instead of secularizing church activities, this has taken away the temptation from the church to deal with secular things. It must be recognized that the program of the church receives greater limitation in this process and that fewer things remain for the church to do. This would not be disturbing to many church leaders if it were not for the fact that, in order to build and maintain a sense of relationship to groups and institutions today, it is necessary for people to be together at times other than the worship service.

(3) While the individual minister has been called upon to counsel with many people regarding their ills during the depression, the rooting of these ills in unemployment and the recognition of the fact that there is very little that the individual as an individual can do about it has driven the minister to think on the major issues of the times, political and economic. He may seek to give these subjects a spiritual orientation but the content of his messages is pushed out of the Biblical and ec-

---

[5] See Barrett, C. B. "A Community WPA Program Centered in Education." *School Board Journal.* Pp. 51ff. April 1937, for an excellent statement of the program provided for an industrial community of 8,000. In this community a liberal church was planning an extensive community program when the depression came. The church group now sees in operation a much more elaborate program than it could have financed. More than $200,000 will have been spent by July 1, 1937.

clesiastical into the same realm with which government and community agencies are dealing.

(4) A question for study would be whether the reduction of funds for church schools and colleges has continued downward at a more rapid rate since the depression began. To the extent that this has occurred, the educational function of the church has been further secularized.

(5) There has been a definite recognition of the fact that relief and philanthropy have moved into a place where the state and the larger community are necessary to meet the demands. The government has taken a much greater share in the various forms of social welfare and social security since the coming of the depression. This has further limited the work of the church. Even before the depression, however, much of the early philanthropic work of the church had been assumed by such organizations as the United Charities, etc.

(6) Church hospitals have taken on the character of community hospitals.

(7) Lack of funds has compelled some churches to use the ways of the community at large to raise funds. These ways are often in sharp contrast with the way in which churches have in the past raised their money.

3. Some Factors Which May Have Slowed Down Secularization During the Depression

(1) Even before the depression struck, Protestant church groups were beginning to realize that they were spending a great deal of money in secular work which seemed to bring them slight returns in terms of membership. Even before the depression, missionary funds had begun to decrease, the church school enrollment had decreased, and churches seemed to be having difficulty in securing attendance. With the coming of the depression, church boards and denominational groups became even more keenly aware of the fact that they would need to have some

sort of philosophy for deciding how much money they should put into secular work or, as some might say, programs of "doing good" as against the amount which they would put into fellowship or membership building groups.[6] This philosophy was more than a revelation of the fact that money was not available. These considerations began before the depression and, therefore, when the depression came, the process of withdrawing funds from institutional churches and neighborhood houses could take place without so many pangs of conscience on the part of the administrators who were making the decision. Undoubtedly, however, the decrease of funds speeded up the process and in this sense the secularization of urban churches has been retarded.

(2) The defeatism which overcame many liberals in theology, as illustrated in the phrase "the tired liberal," is indicative of the fact that liberalism and reform were oversold. This movement was perhaps more pronounced in Europe than in America, and some people have said that the development of Barthianism, the German dialectic theology, Neo-Calvinism (or whatever term is most adequate), is related to the World War and the trying circumstances which followed, especially for Germany. In some quarters this recognition of the oversold nature of liberalism and the limitations of reform have taken the form of turning to a more orthodox religious orientation. Note especially *Reflections on the End of an Era,* by Reinhold Niebuhr:[7] "In my opinion adequate spiritual guidance can come only through a more radical political orientation and more conservative religious convictions than are comprehended in the culture of our era." In America following a period of overoptimistic liberalism, this defeatism has been related to the World War, to the failure of prohibition, to the depression, and to the complexity of international relationships.

[6] The Congregational-Christian denomination has cut both home and foreign missions in order to establish a Council for Social Action.

[7] New York: Charles Scribner's Sons. 1934. P. IX

(3) There seems to have been, during the depression, a renewed urge on the part of denominations to preserve themselves, which has thrown them back upon their own history and upon an interpretation of the special missions which they have had in the world. This has given them a renewed theological orientation which has opposed the process of secularization. The community church movement does not seem to have taken on renewed energy during the depression. Dr. Edward Scribner Ames, in his lectures at Grinnell, Iowa, in February, 1937, pointed out the dilemma of the modern liberal church when it seeks to become a community church. In order to be a community church, he pointed out, the theological emphasis must not be stressed, but rather, the practical needs of the community must be emphasized.

(4) The definite challenge of the church by nonreligious systems such as Communism and the totalitarian state may have swept great areas of life away from churches, but may also have made the remaining church groups much more conscious of what may happen to them and therefore have been responsible for the intensification of the zeal of the church to maintain itself. Church groups recognize that the totalitarian state leaves no place for religious groups to function in bringing about a better order except through the totalitarian government, which refuses to accept the church as an ally but will accept it only as a subordinate. Something much more than survival activity has been occurring. Church leaders and writers have been going through a process of reorientation on the rôle of the church in modern society, especially with reference to the state.[8]

SOME WAYS IN WHICH THE LARGER TOPIC OF SECULARIZATION MAY BE SUBDIVIDED

Research into the problem of secularization necessarily involves the breaking down of the broad topic into units which

---

[8] See the writings of Niebuhr, Reinhold, and MacMurray, John

can be attacked directly. This refinement of the problem can be achieved perhaps most successfully by limiting the size of the unit studied or by studying specific functions.

1. By Size and Nature of the Unit

(1) There are some students who are bold enough to attempt to look at a whole civilization. Gilbert Murray's *Five Stages of Greek Religion* is a major case study in secularization. Here a whole civilization is taken as the unit. Oswald Spengler's *Decline of the West* makes a similar attempt with reference to Western civilization.

(2) It is possible to study the different denominational groupings. These denominational groups have histories and traditions, they have a personnel which is bound together in some form of organization, and they have their literature. These denominational groupings could be studied over long periods of time and an effort made to observe the trends within them.[9] To illustrate the trend within denominations, one might point to the fact that the Disciples of Christ, with their lack of emphasis upon theology, have been slightly influenced by Neo-Calvinism while Congregationalists and Presbyterians who have been nearer the Reformation theology and who have had more theologians among their ministers, may have been more definitely influenced by this movement—at least this might constitute an hypothesis. Social movements and schools of thought which cut across several denominations such as the Social Gospel movement or the Anti-Secularism movement or the Anti-Liberalism movement, Buchmanism or Fundamentalism, should also be studied.

(3) A further basis for division of the subject might be in terms of the different regions within the United States. These

[9] See works of Sweet, William Warren. *Religion on the American Frontier.* New York: Henry Holt and Co. Vol. I, *The Baptists.* 1931. Vol. II, *The Presbyterians.* 1936. Vol. III, *The Congregationalists.* To be published shortly

regions would be related to different denominations since several denominations are regional rather than national in their distribution of members. It is assumed by some authorities that the "East" (that is, schools and seminaries in the East) has been more greatly influenced by Neo-Calvinism than have schools farther from the East. This may be related to the fact that, in the first place, the Atlantic coast is nearer Europe in culture and in thought and, in the second place, it has had more people who have been dealing with theological subjects. This regional approach might be more fruitful than attempts to see what is happening to the country as a whole, since in this way we might get at some of the factors which are responsible for specific changes.[10]

(4) The individual local church may be studied as a unit in this process.[11] Sufficient institutions could be selected so that one would get something which would approach the sampling process. These samples could be selected with very great care because there are many criteria by which they may be chosen.

(5) Secularization may be studied by considering attitudes of the individual church member.

2. By Study of Functions

A further way in which the subject might be subdivided would be in terms of the functions assumed by the larger community—that is, education, philanthropy and relief, care of health and recreation. In dealing with each of these functions one would need to ask the question, In what way does the church still maintain a hold upon them? Even though the community takes over education, church people as church people may still criticize the work of education and seek to make it conform with their principles. Church groups have a way of maintaining that they may look at any aspect of life which makes

[10] See Appendix A
[11] See Appendix B

either for or against "salvation." The term "salvation" is now given a very broad interpretation by many writers.

In thinking of the topic of health, for example, it is recognized that practically every religion has had an interest in health in some form. The medicine man was once a priest. There has been an application of the methods of modern science to health. With the coming of the work of Pasteur in bacteriology, an emphasis was placed upon pure water and pure food. We might say that this aspect of life has been secularized. At the same time most church people recognize that there is still a basis for the relationship of religion to health in terms of faith and hope and an outlook upon life. Some church groups today go in for spiritual healing. One whole group, the Christian Scientist, has given spiritual and religious significance to the matter of health. Other church groups simply say that the church should be a center for health as against a place for the healing of the body. For some church groups loss of these functions is a definite secularization, whereas in certain liberal churches which are committed to the use of modern science, a renewed interest in the work of science is taken and the religious interpretation is made.

In the study of secularization one must keep in mind the fact that religion by certain groups is being interpreted in terms of "the celebration of life,"[12] and that there is a recognition that the religious experience is always, at the same time, some other kind of experience and therefore the so-called secular aspects of life may be given a spiritual interpretation.[13] F. Ernest Johnson states this position:

> . . . The conviction grows that even those types of experience that are considered most secular have a religious phase when considered in relation to the spiritual aspirations of men. The recent publication of *A*

[12] Vogt, Von Ogden. *Modern Worship*. New Haven: Yale University Press. 1927. Chapter I

[13] Ames, Edward Scribner. *Religion*. New York: Henry Holt and Co. 1929 Chapters I and II

Common Faith by John Dewey, the father of progressive educational theory in America, is an illustration and a confirmation of this trend.[14]

Finally, an interesting hypothesis regarding the relation of the business cycle to change in religion was proposed[15] by Dr. Romanzo Adams of Honolulu. Dr. Adams, who has thought much on these topics, makes the following suggestion regarding the relationship of business and religious cycles and assumes that the business cycle is shorter than the religious.

1. Probably there is a cycle in the changes that take place in the religious experience of a people, but it covers a much longer period than does the business cycle.

2. While the cycle of religious experience is related to economic change, it is not much affected by the short term factors that have so much to do with the cycle of business activity. I should suppose that the economic developments of the last century and a half, affecting the whole field of human relations so profoundly, must bring about a very important change in the field of religion. As I see it this development, if plotted in a curve, would show a fairly steady sweep in one direction, while the business cycle has gone through all the stages of its process several times. If this is true, one should not expect to find any very important correlation between the facts of the depression and the facts of the trend in religion.

3. The economists describe the business cycle pretty successfully because they have a reasonably adequate body of economic theory related to it. I do not know of any theory of religion that seems to serve for a description of the cycle of change in religious experience. I do not even know that the students in this field would accept the view that there is a cycle.

4. I have made an effort to work out a theory of this cycle which involves such readjustment in religious thought and in its moral code and ritual as is necessary from time to time on account of important changes in the organization of human relations. As a condition precedent to such readjustment there is a weakening of respect for the traditional things of religion. That is, in the language of a Catholic friend of mine here in Honolulu, people come more and more to "hold sacred things lightly." This means that there is an increasing social disorganization, a decay of communal morale and, in extreme cases, civilization seems to be threatened. But also it means a degree of freedom to approach prac-

[14] Webber, Herman C. (Ed.) *Yearbook of American Churches.* Association Press. 1935 edition. P. 139

[15] In a personal letter to the writer

tical questions with an open mind—that is to devise ways of life from the standpoint of their utility under the given conditions. This is a secular matter and it may be supposed that most of the inventions turn out to be failures. But people learn by the trial and error method and in time there will come into existence an organization of behavior which works pretty well. To the extent that such behavior is justified on the ground that it is practically advantageous, it is secular and society suffers from the fact that there are so many people whose behavior is not in conformity with the requirements of the new organization. Only as the new ways become old and as the rules acquire sanctity do they exercise a sufficient influence over conduct.

As I see it, the cycle involves a modification of human relationships of such a character that traditional religion is, in relation to some things, unadapted, and associated with this there is a readaptation of religion, the readaptation involving first a decreasing intensity of sentiment in support of tradition and later by a growth of sentiment in support of the new way of life.

If there is a cycle of some such character, it would be more important to study the present situation with reference to our position in the cycle of religious change than to study the minor changes in religion due to the developments related to the business cycle.

If one were to attempt a study of the religious cycle, in America, he would meet with one difficulty at the very start. We are not *one* people but *several*. The social backgrounds of the different sections of our population differ greatly and they have not shared in what we may call the common experience of America long enough to have a common American background. Perhaps we are acquiring such a background, but in the nature of things this is a slow process.

For the present it might be better to consider only certain sections of the population—small enough to be fairly homogeneous. For example, one could consider the Italians of Cicero, the Norwegians of Wisconsin rural communities and small cities, the Baptists of Georgia, the Methodists of Iowa, the Irish of Boston or St. Paul or the Congregationalists of Chicago, or maybe those of some one church.

In the following two chapters research is proposed on the effects of the depression on the message of the church and its programs and activities. In studying these problems it should be remembered that they must be viewed against the general trend in these matters and that the secularization of church activities is perhaps the most important aspect of the long-time trend which must be kept in mind.

Chapter V

The Message

PREACHING and teaching have been historic functions for the church. Fundamental to all its activities and purposes there has always been the church's message to mankind. The messages of churches may be seen in preaching, in classes, in forums, and in many informal ways. It is too limited a conception of "message" to assume that it consists only of the spoken or written word of the minister. Ministers themselves speak of the various ways in which the message may be developed and implemented. They even insist that the lives of the members constitute "living epistles."

What did the depression do to this message of the church? In this chapter the effect of economic privation on sermon content, on religious instruction, on the pronouncements and resolutions of religious organizations, and on religious journalism may be used to give some clews as to the ways in which the church's message has been altered or subjected to new emphasis in the past decade.

The viewpoints regarding what has happened to the messages and teachings of churches, with reference to social, political, and economic issues are quite varied. Very complete studies would need to be made in this field before one could be certain of any generalizations. One thing is certain—the relationship of the church to these issues has had much more discussion in recent times than it has had for several decades.

From a broad point of view the church may be thought of as possessing a dual function in the sense that it serves both the individual church members and the community. These functions may be described as personal and social. The former is the service of the church in giving counsel, comfort, guidance, peace and morale to individual church members. The latter concerns the policy of the church in its relation to the existing social, political, and economic structure. It is definitely recognized that the line of distinction between these two phases of the message of the church is difficult to draw. It is imperative, however, if we make analyses, to have a language which permits us to differentiate the phases of the church's message. Just as we need to think of society and the person as complementary and interrelated, so we need to think of social and personal as complementary. The acuteness of personal need often is the incentive to make changes in the social order. Ministers have very different messages and approaches if analyzed from the point of view of their specific remedies for the ills of life.

It may be expected that both the personal and social aspects of the message of the church have been affected by the apparent trend toward the secularization of church activities and teachings. A study of the effects of the depression on the message must therefore consider the influence of the depression on secularization.[1] Although secularization is more often thought of as relating to the broader church program[2] it may also be considered as an important factor in the teachings of the church.

Perhaps the greatest interest in the effects of the depression on the message of the church may, therefore, be centered around these questions: Did the message become more personal or more social? Did it bcome more sacred or more secular? There are many theoretical possibilities implicit in a series of questions on this topic. In thinking, for example, of just two variables we would find that the message might be more sacred and more personal or more sacred and more social. It might be more

[1] See Chapter IV
[2] See Chapter VI

secular and more personal or more secular and more social. These varying combinations might be made with each characteristic of the message studied.

Another fundamental interest in the message of the church centers about the character of its social teachings. During the depression the political, economic, and social attitudes of the government, the business man, the worker, and the public in general were subjected to severe strains. Many traditional policies were modified or abandoned. It is unlikely that the attitudes of the church members and of the clergy were not also affected since church members are also citizens and members of the community. People cannot compartmentalize their lives completely. Was the social, political, and economic message of the church during the depression more reactionary, conservative, neutral, liberal, or radical? Elusive as this question may be for purposes of research, it is clear that it embraces a problem of great interest and importance—one which warrants investigation by whatever methods are available.

Within the general framework established above, the church message might well be expected to vary in accordance with a number of personal and social factors such as the following: the severity with which the depression affected church finances and the clergy; the economic status of the church membership; the urban, rural, and regional characteristics of the church; the political affiliation of church officers, clergy, and lay members; the strength of the trend toward secularization at the onset of the depression; the extent to which the church was influenced by revivalistic or other religious crosscurrents of thought at the onset of the depression. Suggestions for examining these factors are presented later in this chapter.

The broad framework established above will serve, it is hoped, to define the problem and to delineate general lines of investigation. A profitable approach to research in this field would consist in breaking down the broad problems described into specific problems which are amenable to research. Some of the more important questions which can be raised follow:

QUESTIONS AND HYPOTHESES ON THE EFFECTS OF THE DEPRESSION ON THE MESSAGE OF THE CHURCH:

1. Did the Depression Make the Message of the Church More Social Rather Than More Personal?

Obviously materials may be assembled on both sides of this question since in reality the question needs to be put in the following form: in what situations and circumstances did the messages of churches become more social rather than more personal and in what situations did they become more personal?

The very great personal needs of people during the depression led many ministers to seek to meet these needs in interviews. The testimonies to this effect are abundant.[3] The sermons, the spoken messages, were, however, in many instances turned more in the direction of the social because of the obvious fact that the major causes which had forced people into the most trying experiences of their lives were in the great social and economic world which was beyond their own immediate personal control. It may be that these facts stood out more sharply in this depression than in any previous one.

A question for study under this topic would be whether or not the defeats and disappointments of the well-to-do made for more susceptibility to such developments as the Oxford Group Movement. The Oxford Group Movement has been described by John M. Versteeg[4] as a holiness movement for the socially favored. Very often the holiness movements have ministered to the socially underprivileged. The Oxford Group Movement has put the emphasis upon the emotional as against the in-

---

[3] This is frequently referred to in the personal correspondence of clergymen with the author.

[4] *Christian Century*. January 23 1935

tellectual, upon the personal as against the social. Versteeg in the reference given says: "Wesley and his holy club started with social redemption, and then worked out to individuals. But the social concept never entered the minds of the Buchmanites until its critics put it there. And it is there now only as a kind of imitation."

The Oxford Group Movement began before the depression. The question would be whether or not the depression helped or hindered the movement.

2. Has the Depression Made the Message of the Church More Secular Rather Than Sacred? Has the Trend in the Secularization of the Message of the Church Been Speeded Up during the Depression?[5]

There is much evidence for either side of this question. The evidence is clear that some of the work which churches have performed in local communities has been taken over by other agencies but the depression seems to have sharpened the ideological divisions, i.e., the denominational messages of churches in some instances. This would make the messages more denominational, more orthodox, and likely less secular.

In view of the fact that the terminology of sacred and secular arose in the time of a world view very different from our own, perhaps the wording of this proposition should be changed. Some modern writers[6] take the position that the sacred really means that which is central and vital and that the sacred may be found in all phases of life. For many people experiences which are central to life and have deep emotional tone may not be thought of as religious but would be if they were only in the frame of reference of an earlier age. The very fact that we seek

[5] See Chapter IV for a discussion of secularization

[6] Ames, Edward Scribner. *Religion.* New York: Henry Holt and Co. 1929. Chapters I and II

a new language indicates that a major shift has taken place in our thinking.

Secularization represents a long-time trend in which many aspects of life have become no longer the special province of the church but are recognized to be the obligation of the entire community. Illustrations of this are found in education, philanthropy, relief, and hospitalization. The most outstanding development in this general field in recent years has been the assumption by the state of increased obligation to care for the whole of life. The totalitarian state is thought of by the adherents of religion as so completely taking over the loyalties of its citizens that there remains little possibility for the church to function.[7]

Churches have assumed that their function is to give definition and interpretation to the meaning of life. But today numerous philosophers and journalists assume the rôle of the prophet and the interpreter.

3. Did the Depression Speed Up a Movement Away From "Liberalism"?

The term "beyond liberalism" has been used in two main ways. Some use the term to mean more humanistic and less theistic. Many humanists have maintained that the usual position of humanism is not radical enough, that the advocates of this position have not gone far enough. There has arisen another group which says that it is "beyond liberalism," and which believes that the movement must be toward a more definitely theistic position. This second group regrets that the general trend of liberalism has weakened the acceptance of the theistic position. Union Theological Seminary and other eastern theological seminaries have, in recent years, emphasized a more conservative theological position. The result has been to turn

[7] See Oldham, J. H. *Church, Community and State.* London: Student Christian Movement Press. 1935. Pp. 9, 10. The World Conference in Life and Work at Oxford, July 1937, was set up to discuss these questions.

theological thought back toward the Calvinistic-Lutheran viewpoints.

From "Worship and Theology" by the Rev. George M. Gibson of Webster Groves, Missouri, printed in *The Seminar Quarterly* for February 1937, the following excerpts are of particular interest:

This is a plea for a Protestant scholasticism. It may not be invented by a brilliant mind, nor hammered out by a committee in a few sessions. It must come by grant of God as men make themselves ready to receive it.

But, come it must, if we are to experience the "recovery of worship," need for which has so long been felt. For it was Liberalism's anti-theological temper that marked the decline and fall of worship in Protestantism.

The main marks of that culture called "modernity" were: monistic naturalism, excluding whatever reality had theretofore been sensed under the term "supernatural"; materialism with its corollary distrust of primary spiritual reality; optimistic belief in the self-containment of human nature, with its homocentric emphasis; and an arrogant secularity which could witness with glee the procession of "lost provinces" formerly claimed as sanctities.

The self-sufficiency of man was the corollary proposition. . . .

We can no more than indicate the main lines of that scholasticism, and in that indication it will be seen how far afield the modern spirit has wandered from the essentials of fruitful faith.

God: Creator of all things, and as God of love, judge and grace-giver. He is transcendent and objective as Sovereign Lord. "The power not ourselves that makes for righteousness"; He is immanent as Indwelling Spirit.

Christ: the entrance of God into history in redemptive action.

Man: Creature of God and subject to his authority.

Redemption: Man is saved, not by his own righteousness but the free gift of God's grace accepted by faith, after penitence and evidenced by good works.

Church: Ordained of God, it is holy and catholic; essential to man's spiritual welfare and he may not be redeemed beyond its pales; pattern of the redeemed society through cooperative love; it is in the world but not of it, confronting the world as lost, but meeting it in compassion, and in love showing forth the judgment of God on all anti-social elements of society and the grace of God which is the social hope of redemption.

World: the world is evil and lost.

Final Things: The life eternal; the transiency of the unseen world and its institutions; the permanency and ultimate victory of the unseen world; the consequent dualism and the cataclysmic contrast. This is the Christian's dynamic for good works and his inspiration to high fortitude in the face of visible hostile power.

4. Did the Depression Accelerate the Development of the German Dialectic Theology in the United States?

This topic falls within the general discussion of liberalism and of secularization. It might be thought of as a counter movement.

The depression of the 1930's came as a definite challenge and shock to those who had pinned their faith on individual initiative, one of the basic principles of liberalism. If democracy could not succeed in America, the land of plenty and of opportunity, where could it succeed? Moreover to what might men turn? One would expect that this would be the more orthodox position in religion—to the "grace of God," to the idea that the church must always remain against the world. These ideas were developed in America. The question is: to what extent and how deeply did they penetrate? All such developments cannot be traced to Barthianism. Barthianism is itself in the historic Christian tradition. Other groups have ideas similar to Barthianism.

The German dialectic theology, in contrast with the position of liberalism, emphasizes the inability of man to make the world over. Man must wait upon God and God is the completely other than man. The social gospel group emphasized the immanence of God and man as the instrument of God. This position has been so widely accepted that strict Barthianism, as such, likely received very slight acceptance in America. The general emphasis, however, which Barthianism makes, is undoubtedly penetrating many messages in the form of comfort to the individual in his despair of remaking the whole society into "the kingdom of God." It isn't Barthianism as a cult which is penetrating; many ministers are leaning in this direction without having heard of Barth. The same major influences which produced the

Barthian Movement have prepared the ground for the same general emphasis in America. Many ministers at the top of the profession have sensed the "correction" of such an emphasis.

Some guide questions (rather than schedule questions) for the analysis of documents on the retreat from liberalism and the return to the Calvinistic-Lutheran or Reformation theology,[8] emphasis of which Barthianism is one illustration, follow:

(a) Is there definite opposition to the thought that man may make progress and an emphasis upon man's impotence to help himself, or is there emphasis upon man's initiative and ability to achieve progress?

(b) Is man's sinfulness or his natural goodness emphasized?

(c) In statements regarding God, is there an emphasis upon His "holy, totally or completely otherness" as essential to His Being, or is there emphasis upon His immanence and man's ability to share the divine? (This question is especially applicable to Barthianism and does not apply to all those who tend toward a Reformation theology.)

(d) Is there an emphasis upon revelation in which "the word of God and Christ" have special significance and are not understood by orthodox Protestants, or is there emphasis upon the more natural process of inspiration in which it is assumed that man can give a rational interpretation to God's message to man?

(e) Is Christianity emphasized as "the truth" and is religious fraternization and our ability to learn from other religions minimized, or is there a recognition of the good in other religions (such as is found in Re-Thinking Missions)?

5. Was the Message of the Church Influenced by the Economic Conditions of Its Members?

In considering this question it should be remembered that

[8] The term "post liberals" is sometimes used to indicate this group of preachers. These preachers have lost a naïve faith in liberalism but they recognize the "myth" nature of much of Barthianism.

there is a very broad basis for the changes in attitudes of religious and non-religious people. Certain political developments in Europe have, for example, greatly influenced religious viewpoints. Any one of the factors influencing the messages of the clergy was always operating with other factors. The economic condition did not operate alone but always with concomitant factors. While the message is probably influenced by economic situations, a simple economic determinism does not exist. In general, however, it seems reasonable to posit the following hypothesis for investigation:

The social message of churches during the depression was influenced by the economic status of its members and by changes or contemplated changes in the economic situation of the membership and constituency.

This hypothesis can be refined and further subdivided for purposes of research into the following working hypotheses, for purposes of verification or refutation.

(a) The financial pressure on churches, occasioned by the depression, forced many of the clergy to adjust sermons and conduct to the attitudes of the members who could pay the fixed charges of the church. This reaction may have been most pronounced in churches of wealth. These adjustments may have been made by: turning to orthodox or personal religious subjects; taking conservative social and economic positions; by both.

(b) In churches with middle class, working class or farm membership not severely affected by the depression, the message showed little change from predepression days. The discussion of the social issues was in the vein of "academic" or nonaction attitudes.

(c) In churches with middle class, working class or farm membership severely affected by the depression, the message became more liberal or radical economically, more social rather than more personal, and more secular rather than more "religious" in those cases where any relationship of church to life was maintained.

(d) In churches with composite membership, the message fluctuated but for the most part remained on neutral territory.

(e) Where ministers refused to yield to the demands of the more economically and politically conservative members, there developed a rift between clergy and laity.

(f) The influence of the message of the church upon political and economic affairs may have been weaker in this crisis than in previous times. (It would be difficult to answer this proposition either positively or negatively.)

The author's correspondence has yielded some frank and illuminating hints on these points. As expected, the many letters obtained reveal great divergence of opinion among laymen and the clergy on the character and the extent of the influence of economic pressure on the message of the church.

On the one hand, it is said, for example, that many ministers have been willing to keep peace on current political and economic issues at the price of silence and softness. Many writers point out that the debts which churches incurred in boom days have made it necessary for the minister to refrain from speaking his convictions freely. It is suggested by some that a few ministers have added an emphasis to the authoritarianism of religious positions and the will of God because these statements were pleasing to the older, wealthy members of the church. It is assumed by others that there has been a noticeable return to religion by many well-to-do people who look upon the church as a means of preserving the status quo. This position does not seem to be widely held. It may be a correct explanation of the behavior of some people. The important question for further study would be to determine the size of the group to which it applies. Still others make a more generous interpretation, saying that the disappointments of the War, the failure of prohibition, and the coming of the depression drove ministers themselves to fall back upon a more orthodox position and in sincerity, they now emphasize the understanding of the nature of God and the more devotional life. Some ministers taking this general position go so far as to say that no general improvement can be made in the world. For them the church is "against the world," and always must be. They do not hesitate to "do good" but they have lost faith in "reform."

On the other hand, a contrasting view is also found in the author's correspondence. It is widely assumed that ministers in denominations where a considerable number of the members are seeking to preserve the status quo have been more radical politically and economically than have their leading laymen and that there has been a rift between clergy and laity on these issues. These rifts were spoken of openly and in some cases conscious efforts were made to close them. What are the situations in which preachers preach against the tide? In what situations are they able to do so and survive? Where does the rift come? Under what circumstances are ministers permitted to preach ideals which cannot be achieved?

Were the laymen content with radical doctrine as long as church people only talked, but alarmed and full of protest as soon as they saw even a few people attempt to put into practice some of their resolutions? One might analyze the revolt of the Methodist laymen on this score. Church people are accustomed to have the preaching quite at variance with their practice. The argument is made that a minister would not be permitted to say the things he says if he ever expected to be taken seriously. One woman said regarding her minister's address on a theological question: "Oh, it does Dr. X so much good to say those things and they don't hurt me." Is this what many laymen are accustomed to think regarding the pronouncements of churches on economic issues?

In many of the poorest communities where one would expect the most radical reaction, very divergent forms have occurred. The people either accepted an over-emotional and "other worldly" gospel and separated sharply the religious from the worldly, or they turned from the church, and their advocacy of Communism, Socialism, the Townsend Plan, the Share-Your-Wealth Club, and the League for Social Justice took on the characteristics of religious zeal, in some cases with definite antagonism toward the church.

An interesting hypothesis in the field of attitudes toward social reform has been formulated by Dr. Ernest T. Krueger in a personal letter to the writer, which goes deeper than economic well-being. Economic welfare may be basic but the entire question of the security of the person is involved. From the viewpoint of social psychology, security is one of the fundamental aspects of personality; an aspect which is related to the entire "self." This hypothesis relates the fears of the person to basic attitudes:

> During periods of upswing of prosperity and well into the downswing of the depression, church members are conscious of injustices, inequalities, corruption and suffering in the social order and react toward protest and toward social action. But as the depression weaves on its dismaying way, revealing a serious dislocation in social organization, a serious lack of capacity to make economic adjustments and changes to meet the new situation, and a political ineptitude in dealing with issues, a sense of insecurity, a feeling of futility, and inability to think through a solution, arises in the population which suffers but is not severely affected economically with the depression. This part of the population is middle class and hence in our churches, especially our Protestant churches, it begins to feel the need of a mental and emotional security, of an inner personal need of unity, tranquillity and certainty. It therefore desires and demands a form of preaching which feeds the personal life amidst a broken and disturbed social order.

The problems inherent in these hypotheses are in a sense the most vital ones which arise in considering the effects of the depression on the church. It is clear that these questions are in the main not amenable to quantitative research, although something of a quantitative character can be attempted. Unsatisfactory as case and survey materials may be in this field, however, it should be profitable to pursue such investigations for whatever illumination they may cast.

6. The Social Message of Churches During the Depression was Influenced by the Political Attitudes of Their Membership

During the course of this depression many of the most pressing problems became political issues on which the general public had some opportunity in the national elections of 1932 and 1936 to express an opinion. Moreover, the "New Deal" administration, by its vigorous and dramatic action, captured the imagination of large sectors of the public and created widespread enthusiasm about the rôle that the government was playing. Political affiliation during the course of this depression possessed a real significance with respect to pressing national problems of a type unparalleled in recent years in the field of national politics. It seems reasonable to assume that this political enthusiasm and widespread identification with the policies of the government in Washington had some influence on the attitudes of both church officialdom and membership. These effects might be investigated in the framework of the following questions:

(a) In churches with dominantly Republican membership was the message more conservative than in churches of similar circumstances economically but of Democratic membership? (The South must, of course, be treated as a separate unit in this respect.)

(b) Where church members were strongly Democratic did ministers find an easier time advocating social reform?

(c) In churches with mixed Republican and Democratic membership was the message more neutral?

(d) Did some church groups hold back from following the lead of the government and from accepting help because they feared that they would lose their independence?

There is some evidence that congregations which were primarily Republican in political affiliation were somewhat confused by some of the "New Deal" principles which closely resembled the social gospel to which they were accustomed.[9] Some clergymen have indicated that the government's position on social reform made it easier for them to take more definite stands on political and economic problems than was possible prior to the depression.[10] This may have been particularly true in churches in which the congregations were largely Democratic. In such cases it seems clear that the message of the church tended to be more liberal or radical. Finally there is some evidence that some church groupings feared to follow the lead of the government because they would endanger the principle of separation of church and state. Their fears of possible loss of independence were related to the growth of the totalitarian state in Europe. This attitude seems to have been stronger in groups with Republican leanings than it was in groups with Democratic traditions.

In this connection the question might well be raised as to what effect upon the preaching of the social gospel has been exerted by the espousal by the government of so many aspects of the social creeds of the churches.[11] Has the government, in stating its program in such idealistic terms "stolen the thunder" of the churches which advocated a social gospel? On the other hand, have certain church people who have been opposed to the New Deal opposed any social teachings which sound like it? Both President Roosevelt and Secretary Wallace have used the language of the church. The Good Neighbor League has advertised

---

[9] See Stelzle, Charles, *The Social Ideals of the Churches and the Social Program of the Government.* Washington, D. C. Munsly Bldg.: The Good Neighbor League, Inc. 1936. This point also occurs in personal correspondence.

[10] Based on personal correspondence.

[11] Note the pronouncements of the Federal Council of Churches of Christ in America (1908 and 1932), the Encyclical Letter of Pope Leo XIII (1891), and of Pope Pius XI, "Reconstructing the Social Order" (1931), and the elaboration of the encyclical by the Social Action Department of the National Catholic Welfare Conference, and by the acceptance of the Social Ideals of the Central Conference of American Rabbis, the Union of American Hebrew Congregations, and the Rabbinical Assembly of America.

the fact that there is a close correspondence between the social ideals of the churches and the social program of the government.

EFFECTS OF THE DEPRESSION ON TEACHING IN THE SEMINARIES AND THEOLOGICAL SCHOOLS[12]

Another interesting line of investigation would be a study of the effects of the depression on teaching in seminaries and theological schools. A study might be made of the enrollment in various types of courses. Such studies might aim at gauging the influence of the depression on the future message of the church and on the message of the clergy educated during the trough of the business cycle. Some writers take the position that Barthianism and related schools of thought have had greater prominence in theological seminaries than they do in the church at large. If this is so, it is possible that the influence of the depression in increasing the return to a more conservative theological position will extend into the future through the present generation of theological students.

SOURCES OF DATA

It is obvious that at the present time quantitative studies for the conclusive testing of the hypotheses posited and problems outlined would be difficult if not impossible. At this stage of the business cycle research into the effects of the depression on the message of the church is, to a large extent, necessarily dependent on the materials, statistical and otherwise, published, unpublished, and in the memories of the persons associated with the church during the depression—the clergy, church officers, church membership, and teachers and students at seminaries. Some of the more fruitful sources of data are the sermons of ministers and the church school literature, the official church pronouncements or resolutions, and religious literature, including edi-

[12] See *The Education of American Ministers.* New York: Institute of Social and Religious Research. 1934. 4 vols.; see especially May, Mark A. *et al.* Vol. III. "Institutions that Train Ministers."

torials, articles, and news. Much of the data for investigation into this problem must come, however, from questionnaire[13] and case studies based on correspondence or interview and from surveys of denominational groups in their regional and cultural settings and of individual churches in their local settings.

The two most fertile general sources of materials for the study of the message are the religious journals and church pronouncements. These are described in some detail in the following sections:

1. Religious Journals

Religious journalism has chronicled the great sermons and resolutions of recent years. There might well be an analysis of theological literature of a more serious and basic sort to discover if there is any relationship between changes in theological thought and the period of the War, the post-war period and the depression years. The most available and complete materials on these subjects are in religious journals; although some newspapers, as the *New York Times,* print verbatim excerpts from sermons.[14] In religious journals may be found the messages which are representative of the major religious groups—Catholic, Protestant, Jewish—and of the denominations and divisions within each major group. An analysis of the sermons of the Roman Catholic church could not be so readily made from religious journals but much material would be available.[15]

The outstanding liberal religious journal appearing weekly is *The Christian Century,* which has recorded in its pages during these times great numbers of articles, editorials, and sermons bearing directly on the depression and reflecting something of

[13] See Chapter III for proposed questionnaire of type which is also applicable here.

[14] Newspapers such as the *New York Times* are highly selective of their material but hypotheses might be formulated on the basis of the study of such materials.

[15] A list of Roman Catholic journals is to be found in *The Catholic Periodical Index.* New York: The H. W. Wilson Co.

the stages through which we have gone. While *The Christian Century* is a liberal journal of religion, it welcomes statements of various shades of opinion on critical issues. Its materials, however, almost always fall within a certain range. *The Christian Century Pulpit* in which appear seven or eight sermons each month is a very excellent supplement to *The Christian Century* in providing sermons within the general liberal framework. *The Christian Century* has become an interdemoninational journal but is edited by Charles Clayton Morrison who belongs to the Church of the Disciples of Christ. In order to see the richness of material in any one denomination, one might continue to think of the material provided by the Disciples of Christ. There is *The Christian Evangelist,* published in St. Louis, Missouri, which is a kind of orthodox, middle-of-the-road journal. There is also *The Christian Standard* which is definitely conservative, clinging to the early Disciples tradition in a legalistic fashion. Then there is also *The Restoration Journal,* the journal of the still more fundamentalistic group called Church of Christ, which split off from the Disciples. Within one grouping there are four journals representing different positions. Samples could be taken from these and analysis made of the response of each to the depression.

In addition to these more formal and regular journals there are numerous state papers and local organs in which sermons appear. There is also a very great abundance of literature produced for young people's societies in which sermon material is presented. The church school literature which is produced in abundance in every one of the major denominations contains many references to the times in which we live. Furthermore, any one who sits in the church school classes knows very well how, even though a scriptural text of ancient Israel is the basis of the Sunday-school lesson, the teacher, after a few remarks regarding the characters in the lesson, makes an application of the problems to the times in which we live.

The abundance of literature in each one of the groupings is quite sufficient to provide the basis for studies of denominational conditions. This applies to the Jewish groups and the Roman Catholic church as well as to the numerous branches within Protestantism.

There is one clear case of the direction of literature on a significant scale by one denomination which took seriously the problems of the depression, namely the Congregationalists. The setting up of the Council for Social Action provided the means also for the journal, *Social Action.* The list of titles of the issues of this magazine indicates how completely this group has dealt with the depression and with modern social problems. There has been a wide distribution of these materials not only to ministers but also to clubs and classes and social action committees within local churches. The materials have been so sharply put that, in some instances, they have drawn fire from the more conservative members of the congregation. In one church, for example, action was taken which removed the literature table from the foyer.

A partial list of the topics covered by *Social Action* follows:

Within the Law: The Story of the Insull Empire
America in the Depression and Under the New Deal
Peace Plebiscite Edition
Towards an Understanding of Mexico
Armistice Issue
Churches in Social Action: Why and How
The Constitution and Social Issues
America's First Peace Plebiscite
Goals for 1936, Peace, Security, Freedom
Liquor Control
Will the Church Demand Racial Justice?
Profits and the Profit System
Some Facts about Farming
Christianity and the Cooperatives
Churches at Work in Social Action
The Textile Primer
Gains for Middle Groups Through Social Reconstruction
Youth Organizes to Gain Rights
Problems of Organized Labor

Democracy and the Negro
Campaign Issues: 1936
War and the Christian Church
Social Security in America
This Question of Relief
Girls in Reform Schools
Child Welfare
Spain: Battleground of Democracy
Social Action Primer
Towards a New America
Why Did the Auto Workers Strike?
Good Housing for America
Is Health the Public's Business?

It would be instructive to have a classification of the publications of each of the principal denominations and religious groups in America. The amount of publication by religious groups seems to be enormous.[16]

2. Pronouncements and Resolutions

Roman Catholic Pronouncements

The wide variety of the general pronouncements of the Roman Catholic church during the depression could be studied from documents and speeches. The Quadragesimo Anno Encyclical Letter of Pope Pius XI on "Reconstructing the Social Order" (issued May 15, 1931)[17] discusses, among other things, workingmen's unions, associations of employers, the authority of the church in social and economic spheres, the right of property, the obligations of ownership, the power of the state, obligations regarding superfluous income, capital and labor, unjust claims of capital, unjust claims of labor, the principle of just distribution, the uplifting of the proletariat, just wages, the individual and social character of labor, the support of families, the common good, the social order, harmony in society, strikes and lock-

[16] See Chapter VI on "Program and Activities" for comments on church school materials.

[17] New York: Paulist Press. 401 W. 59th St.

outs, socialism, communism, moral renovation, the loss of souls, and the course to be followed in all these problems.

Special application in various fields has been made of the Encyclical Letter of Pope Pius XI, "Reconstructing the Social Order." Rev. R. A. McGowan of the Social Action Department, National Catholic Welfare Conference, did it for agriculture in an address delivered before the Catholic Conference on Industrial Problems at the 1931 Catholic Rural Life Conference, Wichita, Kansas.[18]

Pronouncements of the Federal Council of Churches of Christ in America

This national, central organization of American Protestantism has been active in attempting to state the position of the church toward its social and economic environment.

In specific fields the Federal Council of Churches of Christ recommends to its Protestant constituency in various of its pamphlet publications what local churches can do in social service and industrial relations.[19] In 1934, a message to the churches[20] called for a frank evaluation of their shortcomings and the necessity for new commitments to Christ, to Christian social ideals, and to a renewed personal devotion in life.

The Federal Council of Churches of Christ published "The Social Creed of the Churches" in 1908 and again in 1912. The new social creed of the churches was adopted at Indianapolis at the meeting of the Federal Council of Churches December 8, 1932.

[18] *Catholic Action.* November 1931, and January 1932. The National Catholic Welfare Conference, 1312 Massachusetts Avenue N.W., Washington, D.C., doubtless would have the best bibliography of literature in this field.

[19] *What Your Church Can Do in Social Service and Industrial Relations.* New York: The Commission on the Church and Social Service of the Federal Council of Churches of Christ in America

[20] "A Message for the Churches." Adopted by the Biennial Meeting of the Federal Council of Churches of Christ in America, Dayton, Ohio. December 4-7 1934

Congregational-Christian Pronouncements

There has been much debate on the part of church people who are in the business and industrial world of the action of the General Council of Congregational-Christian Churches taken in Oberlin in 1934. Definite organization and funds were provided for "social action" which seemed to imply something more than general information. It suggested that specific situations could be studied and afford a basis for "social action." A Council of Social Action with a good-sized budget and a staff of at least six people was provided. There was a general secretary, an associate secretary, a secretary on industrial relations, one on rural life, a research secretary and a secretary on community work, together with secretarial help and funds for the publication of a magazine called *Social Action.*

Dr. Arthur E. Holt, then Chairman of the Council for Social Action, wrote an article for the Congregational constituency[21] on "What the Council for Social Action Proposes."

Methodist Pronouncements

The Northern Methodists have supplied the basis for much discussion. Under pressure of financial commitments, they seemed to retreat from their earlier, more advanced social and economic positions. Some of the more radical secretaries were relieved of their work. The young people were up in arms. There was a question whether or not the National Council of Methodist Youth would decide to sever its connection with the general conference of the Methodist church. The Council remained in the church but had no difficulty in issuing "virtually unanimous criticisms of the church" in resolutions passed at Berea, Kentucky, September 20, 1936. This resolution came from Methodist young people after a prominent group of Methodist laymen had entered the controversy and issued interesting statements of their point of view on this matter.

It would be interesting and valuable to study the Methodist

[21] *Advance.* September 20 1934. P. 494

resolutions from the various sections of the country. These resolutions are to be found in printed form in the various conference and yearbooks.

Presbyterian Pronouncements

Official pronouncement of the General Assembly of the Presbyterian Church of the U.S.A.[22] dealing with social and industrial relations are among the most complete and detailed made by any major denominations. The statements cover the topics of Christian obligation, competition and cooperation, democracy in industry, wages, the right to work and organize, the profit motive, hours of work and employment of women, protection of the family, child labor and child welfare, justice for the farmer, conditions of machinery, industrial accidents, disease and unemployment, housing and health, social insurance, war, and similar issues of social concern. The statements made in 1934 and 1935 reflect a growing concern in these matters and more positive statements of the church's attitude.

Pronouncements of Other Religious Groups

The historic position of the Lutheran church with reference to church and state has doubtless been largely responsible for the fact that one is unable to find many significant resolutions by Lutheran bodies on social and industrial problems. More complete study should be made of the trends which are undoubtedly beginning in this field. The Baptists made very similar resolutions but without as much organization or as many funds.

In the Jewish groups there have been pronouncements by various rabbinical associations. Mr. Louis Minsky, in an article entitled "Rabbis and Social Justice,"[23] says: Coincidentally with the opening of the Jewish New Year the Central Conference of American Rabbis issued a profoundly significant statement on

[22] Official Pronouncements of the Presbyterian Church in the U.S.A., Presbyterian General Assembly, Witherspoon Building, Philadelphia, Pennsylvania.

[23] *The Christian Century.* October 7 1936

social justice which virtually called upon Jews to be prepared to suffer martyrdom in bringing to pass a better social order."

Finally, it should be interesting to study the pronouncements of the many minor religious groups.

SUGGESTIONS FOR RESEARCH

Until recently the method of determining changes in theological thought has been that of personal evaluation in the fashion of the historian, the theologian, or the philosopher. The individual historian, philosopher, or theologian has striven for an impersonal and objective attitude toward the data, but the "personal equation" is difficult to eliminate.

Perhaps some categories of analysis on a scale or continuum[24] might be developed on the basis of which three or five men could come to have a universe of discourse which would permit them to go beyond the evaluations made by the single individual. A problem in the application of statistical procedures in this field would be in determining with what unit to deal. If it is small, the real meaning of the entire document may be lost; if it is large the study would be less exact. Some device must be found for the treatment of the many currents of thought or positions within a document and if possible for treating documents as a whole. This may be done to best advantage where unusual consistency is found in the sermons studied. Perhaps the beginning of such a study would be the attempt of theologians within the same school of thought to work on the same project and to develop uniform criteria for the analysis which they make. Even this would be very difficult for it often happens that such men have differences of emphasis which, to them, are very important.

Another alternative, to use as a beginning to such a study, would be the employment of social science students who have been especially interested in religion, yet who are not as likely

---

[24] For a statement on the continuum see Bogoslovsky, Boris B. *The Technique of Controversy.* New York: Harcourt, Brace & Co. 1928. Pp. 69-70

as theological students to put too much emphasis on subtle differences between theological positions. This would be an effort to see trends of theological thought in their major outlines and in their major positions. Theologians might not like this procedure because it would do violence to the finer differences of thought to which they have given so much attention. Care would be necessary, of course, lest real differences be unnoticed.

Careful sampling and analysis is necessary to catch the meaning of those ministers who use a language which satisfies members with very different viewpoints. Ministers have very subtle ways of introducing sentences to meet the demanding attitudes of various members of their congregations. The printed sermon is not so subject to these variations and presents a more consistent position. Some ministers establish themselves on a basis which they are willing and able to defend so that they have a consistency of position which permits classification. While ministers may declare themselves with reference to one main item of thought, they may not do so with all. It may be that where a minister finds his position on one topic out of the tradition, he takes pains to conform in other phases of his message.

The variations and shifts in attitudes at various periods during the depression must be kept in mind. The individual ministers at different stages in the depression moved toward and from different positions with reference to (a) the sacred and secular, (b) the personal and social, and (c) the radical or conservative. There is need to keep these temporal variations in mind as we seek to see the more permanent effects of the depression period. It is quite probable, however, that a given minister remained within a general viewpoint. The writer would assume that, while there has been variation of position, there has been relatively little "mutation."

One method for studying sermons, church school materials, religious journals, books, pronouncements, etc., might be that of building a continuum for each hypothesis or item to be considered. It could include the working out of criteria for the determination of placing a man or a document at a certain position.

EXAMPLE OF A STUDY OF THE MESSAGE IN THE DEPRESSION

Mr. Lewis Troyer, a student in the Chicago Theological Seminary, was asked by the writer to attempt a preliminary answer to the question: In what ways, if any, did the depression affect the message of the church, as indicated by sermons and articles in religious journals? Below is a summary of his type of observation and method:

This is an attempt to answer the problem by examining four typical church periodicals for expressions of theology in sermons, major articles and editorials. Data pertinent to the problem shall include at least the following items:

(1) Total number of articles, editorials, sermons examined.
(2) Number of references to the depression or closely related social problems.
(3) Proportion that (2) is of (1).
(4) Catalogue of theological positions taken with reference to the depression or closely related social problems.
(5) Arrangement of these positions on a theological continuum, showing trend of emphasis in each periodical for the period of the depression and, if possible, the total trends.

The period covered is from January 1, 1930 to January 1, 1936. The periodicals examined are *The Christian Century, The Christian Century Pulpit, The Presbyterian Advance-Tribune* and *The Moody Bible Institute Monthly.*

The theological continuum is arranged in such a way that positions to the left represent the primacy of supernatural forces of control in the depression situation and positions to the right represent varying degrees of human control, continuing to the most extreme espousal of human social control.

The hypotheses to be considered are:

(1) The depression was reflected in the theology of the churches, an increased attention having been given to the theological implications of social problems.
(2) The depression tended to force a shift in theology toward the more conservative and supernaturalistic positions, especially the German dialectic.
(3) The depression tended to produce a theological shift toward the

more radical, social and humanistic positions, especially the social gospel.

(4) The depression tended to produce an added emphasis upon typical positions already held, with little if any shift to right or left.

The general conclusions are as follows:

(1) Slight attention was directed toward the depression from a theological standpoint in 1930. Beginning with that year, the number of articles dealing with the depression gradually increased to a peak in 1933, and after that declined gradually. The following exceptions should be noted, however:

(a) Attention reached its peak in *The Christian Century Pulpit* in 1932, but was also high in 1933.

(b) *The Moody Bible Institute Monthly* shows its highest point in 1935, after following the general trend otherwise, but among the articles referring to the depression in 1935 only one-half revealed any discernible theological positions. If this factor is taken into account the percentage again accords with the major trend.

(2) The consistently chief emphasis in *The Moody Bible Institute Monthly* was on the position that suffering, privations, depressions and all manner of catastrophes and troubles are to be taken as signs of the "last days"; the second coming of the Lord is imminent. In the meantime it is the part of men to believe on Him and to preach the Bible. The highest point of this emphasis was in 1933. Other positions recorded were much scattered, but noticeably clustered toward the left side of the continuum. No other periodical examined offered contributions to this position. It, therefore, represents a special theological outlook. As such, it is typical of the Moody fundamentalism, for which the depression simply offered opportunity of expression.

(3) The consistently chief emphasis in *The Christian Century* was upon the position that depressions are due to basic social causes and deep-rooted trends. The situation calls for reconstruction of basic institutions and accepted practices. This must be done by means of social planning, cooperative action, use of organized intelligence, application of Christian ethics to the task of reorganizing attitudes, habits, institutional structures. The highest point of this emphasis was in 1935. Other positions are scattered, but noticeably clustered toward the right end of the continuum. This is, in general, what might have been expected of a periodical representing freedom of expression, especially of liberal and radical positions.

(4) *The Christian Century Pulpit,* reflecting directly the actual preaching of ministers in the pulpit, put its chief and consistent emphasis upon the position that depressions come chiefly because men are not sur-

rendered to Christ personally. Society may be saved only by changing the hearts and minds of individuals. Change in individuals must precede any change in the system of relationships. Other positions are scattered widely over the continuum with the weight just right of the center of the continuum.

(5) *The Presbyterian Advance,* representing a distinct denomination, gave consistently chief emphasis to the position represented by (4) until 1935; at the same time a growing secondary emphasis was placed on position (3).

To fully substantiate the foregoing conclusions, further study should be carried out, particularly with regard to several other denominational publications—a Methodist journal, a Congregational or Episcopal publication and a Lutheran magazine.

This methodology might well be applied to a particular theological point of view. The continuum of positions would need to be constructed with the help of several people acquainted with the field.

BACKGROUND FACTORS THAT MUST BE CONSIDERED

In the collection of source data it is particularly important that adequate controls or methods for holding constant various factors be established and maintained. Control of the economic factor, for example, is afforded by such data as income, census tract rentals (in census tract cities), size of contributions, value of the church plant, the size of the budget, salaries, size of the mortgage, unemployment in the community, the incidence of relief, the amount expended on relief, payroll data, the major industries and major occupations in the community, the economic status and connections of trustees and church officers. Communities where a very high percentage of unemployment exists or has existed, and stranded areas might be regarded as laboratory conditions in which economic pressure is magnified and intensified to a point where its effects on the church message theoretically should be visible.

Political controls can be established on the basis of election results, party affiliations or voting practice as determined through questionnaire or case studies, the political affiliation of the local press, political affiliation of church trustees or officers.

Certain regions and areas within regions are known by past performance to have consistent records.

Personal and social facts about the individual clergyman should also furnish important control data. The rapidity of promotion of the clergyman, his previous record, salary class, education, reading materials, social background, war experience, political attitudes, the size of his family, etc., are important factors in accounting for the character of his message during the depression. The denomination and the minister compete for the place of greatest importance when we think of the variants which determine the message of a particular church.

The characteristics of the community in which the church is located should also be controlled as far as possible. Its size, urban or rural character, regional location, economic base, and relation to other communities may be important variables in influencing the depression effects on the message of the church.

Finally, the denomination of the church should obviously be thought of as a major determining factor. The history and tradition of the denomination in relationship to types of theology and social activities are important. In general, the major groupings will be found to be adequate for control purposes.

To the extent to which the data and method of research make it possible, significant cross-classifications of these items might be attempted. Political affiliation, for example, as a factor in influencing the message of the church during the depression, might well be expected to vary in accordance with the severity with which the depression struck the community, the church, and church members.

Some cases should be set up for study where all factors, except one, are similar, in order to isolate factors which are dominant over others in determining the message. For example, one might hold roughly constant political and community conditions, while the denominational item varies. Regional variations of the messages of ministers of similar economic, political, and denominational background might be revealing if closely studied. At a later time, on the basis of these eliminations, some more exact analysis might be attempted.

If one were studying various items of the message in relationship to the factors just mentioned, it would be an advantage to use census tract cities where very adequate quantification of several important items could be made. The metropolitan region has in it sharper variations than are found between any two metropolitan regions taken as a whole.

By studying a sector of a large city one is able to build base maps, to assemble data, to treat these data graphically and thereby to find the major areas of similarity. One will be on his guard immediately not to jump to conclusions regarding the similarities of communities in a few factors, when one of the maps of a series calls attention to the difference in race or nationality origin which may constitute such a major difference that it demands special treatment.

The Department of Research and Survey of the Chicago Theological Seminary and the Chicago Congregational Union has taken as a major unit of study an entire sector of metropolitan Chicago which has within it great variations in community conditions but where the communities have defined relationships to each other. This permits the study of a major nationality group over a period of time, giving the advantage of seeing the same group in different stages of development.

This brief survey of the problems to be considered in studying the message of the church during a depression indicates that such a study will undoubtedly reveal the church's enlarging interest in social and economic manifestations of this depression, as well as a diversity and division of opinion in its ranks on many of these matters. There is indicated a growing, practical relationship of the church to society as revealed in the church's message to its people in years of trouble and misfortune. There are also evident many phases worthy of study to gauge more accurately the influence and importance of these departures of the church from, or its reorientation to, its theological past.

Chapter VI

Program and Activities

FACED by declining income, harassed by building debts and confronted with the need of enlarged services, greater counseling and discussion of community programs, the changes which the church made in its program, its activities and its structure, under the pressure of the depression, comprise an important set of problems for study. Here we must examine not only possible changes in the actual worship service, but fundamental adjustments in personnel, the church program, incentives to church union, trends toward secularization, and such new interests as cooperatives, which were suggested to churchmen as the depression grew more severe.

Robert S. and Helen M. Lynd in their important restudy of Muncie, Indiana,[1] come to the conclusion that the church did not extend its functions during the depression years in ministering to material needs. They write:

> The main body of churches has continued to accept the fact that care for the unable has become secularized in the office of the township trustee, the Social Service Bureau, and the Community Fund; individual church members are strong supporters of these agencies, but the churches as organizations accept the role of spiritual agents rather than leaders or organizers of group care for the needy.[2]

In this chapter we shall consider some selected broad problems for study. For example:

What did churches and denominations actually do during the

---

[1] Lynd, Robert S. and Helen M. *Middletown in Transition*. New York: Harcourt, Brace & Co. 1937

[2] *Ibid*. P. 306

depression that they did not do before? Which of these new tasks have remained as permanent parts of their work? How have these changes given a different emphasis to what has been done?

What functions of the church tended to be curtailed first and most markedly? This particular point has considerable importance if it enables us to discover by objective means what the church considers essential to religion. What functions were curtailed last or least or not at all?

This study should be approached on the basis of the description of the activities of the church. Some of these changes are reflected in church bulletins of which churches have files. One might seek to note the changes in emphasis before and at different times during the depression. It is quite obvious, for example, that early in the depression churches emphasized the relief needs of members of their churches and communities and that later such work was carried on by the government.

The program of the church embraces the following range of activities:

1. The worship service: the sermon; music; choir.
2. Education: the church school, parochial school, "Christian School"; forums and classes in both religion and topics of community interest, such as economics and civics.
3. Church fellowship and recreational groups: women's and men's clubs; societies; clubs and recreation for young people and children; Boy Scouts, Girl Scouts.
4. Evangelism: local church evangelism.
5. Foreign and home missions: the maintenance of local societies.
6. Philanthropy, relief, and social service.
7. Community service: seven-day week program; institutional churches; neighborhood houses.
8. Special organizations for dramatics, music, etc.
9. Maintenance of the church plant.

Many of these activities can be studied quantitatively through investigation of their financial and membership aspects.[3] Time series can be compiled from the yearbooks, regional reports

[3] See Chapter II, "Church Finances."

(conference, synod, diocese, etc.), and from the annual reports or records of various churches. The amounts of money expended on each of these activities over a period of years might serve as a good index of the general character of the program and activities of the church. It would be necessary, first of all, to establish trends in absolute and proportionate expenditures preliminary to gauging absolute and relative depression and recovery effects. A series of hypothesis might well be posited for the study of depression effects on the church program and activities as measured by church finances. Among these the following could be included:

1. *During the depression foreign and home mission activities were contracted absolutely and relatively more than local activities.*
2. *Activities which involved the services of persons other than the clergy were contracted more than the clerical activities.*
3. *"Secular" activities were contracted more than the more definitely religious ones.*
4. *In spite of the tradition of separation of church and state, there has been large use by church controlled institutions of helpers supplied by the government or community funds.*

A study of the effects of the depression on the church activities enumerated and discussed below should shed light on these hypotheses. In such investigation differentials should be noted in accordance with the relevant factors mentioned above.[4] Any conclusions on the effects of the depression on these activities must be carefully checked, of course, against long time trends so far as they can be constructed.[5]

THE WORSHIP SERVICE

It is very doubtful if any very objective means may be developed for the treatment of the worship service. Dr. E. J. Chave[6] has developed some unpublished forms for its study. The writer maintains that the entire service should be recorded in a narrative

---

[4] See Chapter V, "The Message."

[5] See Chapter IV, "Secularization—General Considerations."

[6] Divinity School, University of Chicago

account, and criteria applied so that other workers may check the analysis made.

One would expect very little change in the form of worship of Roman Catholic, Protestant Episcopal, and certain Lutheran churches during the depression. These groups are long lived and have forms which extend over the centuries. The visitor to these churches during the depression was struck with the contrast between them and the churches of the early American emphasis, such as the Baptist, Congregational, Disciples of Christ, Methodist, and Presbyterian. One could visit the former group without knowing that we were in a depression period while in the latter group one was made very conscious of the times in which we are living. The changes were not in the form of worship so much as in the content of the announcements and the sermon which occupies a very different place in the first as compared with the second group of denominations. The change in content becomes so important that it seems to alter the very structure of the service itself.

In what ways do the basic rituals of a church change? In general, they constitute a kind of unchanging center. How far removed from the vital experiences of life may they become and still remain effective?[7] The rituals of primitive people often have a direct relationship to the crises periods of the group and of the individual. Do major periods of depression constitute the kind of social experience which can bring changes in ritual? If they do so, what processes are involved? Does a change in the content of the sermon have implications for other parts of the service? These are questions which could be answered only on the basis of intensive case studies of churches in the different groups.

EVANGELISM

What has the depression done to evangelism, or what forms

[7] See Morrison, Charles Clayton. *The Social Gospel and the Christian Cultus.* New York: Harper & Brothers. 1933

has evangelism taken during the depression? The Preaching Mission has existed for many years in Roman Catholic and Protestant Episcopal groups. It seems to have had a revival in recent years in those churches which did not make use of it earlier. Has its revival been related to the discouragements of the depression?

Much has been made in some circles of the National Preaching Mission. We must use care in attributing all such moves to the depression. Church leaders try many devices even in times of prosperity. Some groups which have grown weary of reform have fallen back upon the more conventional church practices. In those groups where revivals were common there has been a renewed use in the hope that added strength might be gained. There has been much emphasis on the belief that what society needs is religion. The southern groups which have used revivals and which have emphasized evangelism have increased at a more rapid rate than the northern groups which have made less use of those methods; their birth rates have been higher also. The northern groups which have used "preaching missions" have nurtured their own members but have not added many new members in this fashion.

The trend over the past thirty years has been away from emotional revival services; and the depression does not seem to have produced much variation in this major trend.[8] People have had many emotional outlets in other forms. These other emotional outlets, especially the movies and the radio, have so much variety and novelty as well as appeal to the senses that they may be a large factor in so dividing the attention of people that the revival cannot gain control. This affords one hypothesis as to the lack of renewed interest in either the revival or the more refined forms of evangelism. It must be kept in mind, however, that there was a rather generous response to the National Preaching

[8] ". . . But on the whole, if the number of revivals is any index of religious interest in the depression, there has been a marked recession." From Lynd, Robert S. and Helen M. *Middletown in Transition*. P. 303

Mission conducted by the Federal Council of Churches of Christ in America in the autumn of 1936.

Some writers and speakers are predicting that something like the National Preaching Mission will sweep the country back to religion. The magazine *Time* for December 14, 1936, gave a summary of the National Preaching Mission, and numerous religious journals and daily papers of October, November, and December, 1936 carried comments, descriptions, and evaluations. This preaching mission movement is just now under way and affords an opportunity to study a present day effort to revive religious zeal.

Revivals as a means of securing new church members have declined in number and interest especially in the North. They have declined in the South but are still used[9] in many instances with the local minister as the leader.

Many writers and speakers assume that the old mass evangelistic method has gone. A northern minister in a city of 40,000 writes to the author, "Ordinary revival methods have been tried in church after church and the response is utterly negligible. I think that soon they will be definitely abandoned by all normal church groups." Many looked for the depression to bring revivalism back. There is general agreement that there is little or no evidence that this has transpired.

Has the reaction of people to churches been different in the depression of the 1930's from what it was in previous depressions? At the beginning of the depression there was an assumption on the part of some church people that if the depression continued the country would experience a wave of revivals. Some writers made this proposition on the basis of what they assumed had happened in previous periods of depression.[10] There are

[9] See Sneed, Melvin W., and Ensminger, Douglas. *The Rural Church in Missouri. Research Bulletin* 225. Columbia: University of Missouri. 1935

[10] For a statement of the depression of 1857-58 as the cause of the revival of 1858 see Gaddis, M. E. *Christian Perfectionism in America.* University of Chicago. Ph.D. thesis. 1929

others who assume that religious interest expands during good times.[11]

Those who hold the thesis that depression times have, in the past, "driven men to God" are compelled to admit that this depression did not do so. They may point to the statement that our behavior was characterized as "near religious" and give examples ranging all the way from the phenomena accompanying Father Divine to the emphasis upon "neighborliness" and similar emphases by President Roosevelt and Secretary Wallace.[12] At any rate the churches do not seem to have reaped a large harvest during these lean years of economic life and church leaders agree that "revivalism" is passing away. This has led the editor of *The Christian Century* to inquire whether or not this is a manmade depression, suggesting that this is the first time men have not blamed God for hard times.[13] To quote from the editorial:[14]

> It must be a subject of at least occasional reflection on the part of thoughtful people that this period of depression has brought forth no revival of religion. We are accustomed to expect revivals in such periods. They have regularly come in the past, and from the beginning of the present depression a revival has been persistently predicted, particularly by those who are in some special sense charged with a professional rsponsibility for what is called evangelism.
>
> In former economic calamities, men have tended to regard their suffering as due to forces beyond their control. Hard times sprang mysteriously out of the nature of things. . . . The religious attitude toward such an inexorable situation was, therefore, one of awe and resignation, accompanied by the consciousness that, no doubt, men had offended God and that only by repentance could God be reconciled. It was this belief and mood which underlay all religious revivals in

[11] Schattenmann, Johannes. *The Correlation of Religion and Economics in the History of the United States, 1720-1880.* New York: Union Theological Seminary thesis. May 1929

[12] Wallace, Henry. *Statesmanship and Religion.* New York: Round Table Press. 1934

[13] It is clear from numerous letters received by the author that there are many people, especially in rural parishes of the South, who think of this depression as God-sent because of the sins of the people.

[14] *The Christian Century.* September 18 1935. Pp. 1168-1170

previous depressions. Men in their helplessness were driven by calamity to seek help from God and to make their peace with Him.

But in this depression it is different. The idea is now abroad that so-called economic law is not like the laws of nature. We are no longer under the illusion that our economic system is fixed for us. Among the masses of men, as well as the more sophisticated, the idea prevails that our economic system is a man-made system. And being man-made it can be remade. There are many theories as to how it can be remade, but men are conscious, as they never were in any previous depression, that this depression is unnecessary. It is not an "act of God" like an earthquake, but it is due to the failure of human intelligence or the blind power of entrenched privilege, or both. It is therefore not something about which one need get "religious." What one needs is to become intelligent, rather than religious, and to help unify the power of the unprivileged masses for the setting up of an economic system whose productive processes shall function for human use, not for the profits of a single class.

These are questions upon which it would be difficult to get answers. An hypothesis regarding the extent of the secularization of life and attitudes might arise out of such considerations. The church historians might raise the question: "Is this depression the first to register the secularization of attitude which has taken place over the years, or when did depressions cease to bring revivals—if they ever did bring them?"

THE EDUCATIONAL WORK OF CHURCHES[15]

The educational work of churches during the depression and the effects of the depression on such work should be the subject

[15] Special articles on the effects of the depression on religious education are:

Coe, George A. "The Present Crisis in Religious Education," *Religious Education.* 28:181-185. April 1933

Hartshorne, Hugh. "A Study of the Status of Religious Education," *Religious Education.* 27:245-247. March 1932

Hayward, P. H., English, M. N., *et al.* "What the Depression Is Doing to the Cause of Religious Education" (a symposium). *Religious Education.* 27:873-886. December 1932

Norton, John K. "Education in the Depression." *Religious Education.* 29:9-12. January 1934

See also Hartshorne, Hugh, Stearns, Helen R., and Uphaus, W. *Standards and Trends in Religious Education.* New Haven: Yale University Press. 1933

of a special study. It must be kept in mind that church schools (Sunday schools) constitute only a part of such work even in the Protestant churches of British-American origin. There was a greater use of forums and discussion groups at periods during the depression. There were special committees responsible for various aspects of church work which distribute literature and conduct discussions. It is assumed by many that there has been a trend in the expansion of the educational work of churches especially in the social issues which have arisen in recent times.

What changes have been made in curriculum material during the depression? A preliminary study of the catalogues of church publishing houses reveals the fact that there are changes. In what denominational literature have more social problems been included?

A study of church school literature since 1926 might reveal very significant changes. Certain major basic changes in the curriculum of religious education had been made before 1926. The depression sharpened the conditions which the earlier changes were designed to meet.[16] Here is probably a clear case of the speeding up of a trend already under way. In reading *The Adult Bible Class Magazine,* a magazine which has been published for over twenty-five years, one finds a special writer whose assignment it is to make an application of the lesson to the great social questions of the day. Articles dealing with adult civic education, religion, and politics have had a surprising frankness in them during the depression.[17] Criteria for judging and rating these church school materials could be developed.[18] The great advantage in the use of such material is that it is readily available in libraries and publishing houses. It may reflect in a sort of in-

[16] See Bower, William Clayton. *The Curriculum of Religious Education.* New York: Charles Scribner's Sons. 1925

[17] *The Adult Bible Class Magazine.* Published monthly. Congregational Publishing Society. Boston: Pilgrim Press. (See especially April 1 1934 and November 1936)

[18] See Chapter V, "The Message"

direct fashion trends which are taking place. There are a number of optional courses published which show even greater variation in subject matter and treatment than do the required or regular courses.[19]

The reduced budgets of churches have caused a reduction in the staff. In many cases the first to go has been the director of religious education. It is obvious that in the choice between a pastor and a director, the pastor must stay. The crest of the movement for the use of directors of religious education had already arrived and a recession had begun before the depression struck. The depression, however, greatly accelerated the movement. Some authorities in the field of religious education maintain that the reduced budgets during the depression have made a major shift in the personnel and program of churches in that the director of religious education has, with few exceptions, gone into other forms of work and for some time their places cannot be refilled. There are now (spring of 1937) more calls for directors of religious education than can be filled.[20] The suggestion is made that as the director of religious education returns his function will be different from what it was before the depression.

Intensive studies of the changes in church school (Sunday school) attendance should be made by totals for denominations and for states and sections. There was a decline in church school attendance before the depression set in, partly due, no doubt, to the changing birth rate. There are better figures for church school attendance than for most aspects of the church's work. There should be denominational, regional, and institutional studies since it is clear that many factors are operating in the determination of interest in church school attendance.

Dr. Harlan Paul Douglass has suggested that the attendance at young people's conferences has greatly increased the number of hours which young people devote to religious education.

---

[19] See catalogues of publishers year by year since 1926 for titles and descriptions.

[20] This is the position of William Clayton Bower of the University of Chicago

Figures for these gatherings are not readily available. Dr. Harry Thomas Stock, when asked regarding the groups with which he works, says:

In 1922 when this department was established, there were about a dozen young people's conferences in our own fellowship (Congregational church). The number now varies from forty to sixty, depending upon whether we include those that are not strictly denominational but are inter-denominational in the sense of being set up and promoted through the cooperation of denominational officials. There are about fifty strictly denominational conferences. The enrollment during the last few years has averaged about five thousand. There was no decline during the years of the depression. We noticed last summer that some conferences had fewer boys than was the case during the two or three years preceding; this was due doubtless to the fact that jobs were becoming available once more.

Dr. Arthur E. Holt has said that these young people's conferences are more like the European folk school movement than anything else we have in America. The topics of study not only cover the conventional topics of church schools but include war and peace, international affairs, and social and economic situations.

The Roman Catholic Church and branches within the Lutheran group conduct parochial schools. The Reformed groups maintain their Christian schools which are private schools and not, strictly speaking, parochial schools. An understanding of what went on in all these groups would be of very great interest. Such studies could be made from available materials.[21]

The depression raised questions in many situations about the granting of funds by the state for parochial schools conducted by Roman Catholics. An important effect of these discussions has been the sharpening of attitude between Catholic and Protestant groups. These problems are related to the question of relief funds given directly to Roman Catholic organizations.

Has the depression speeded up the idea that the old-fashioned

[21] See Biennial Survey of Education, Office of Education, Department of Interior, Washington, D.C., for statistics on enrollment, number of schools, number of teachers, size of schools, etc.

Sunday school is outmoded and that a new approach to religious education is necessary? At the present time this question would probably need to be answered by an opinion study with some sort of rating scale.

Has the depression speeded up or retarded the process by which religious groups have been compelled to relinquish control over colleges? This movement was under way before the depression set in. Some small colleges have sought to maintain themselves on cooperative plans. The local clientele of colleges has been increased during the depression.

It seems that those overhead organizations in the field of religious education which were most closely tied in with the regular on-going program fared better than those which were marginal to the actual operation.[22]

FOREIGN MISSIONS

For centuries churches have insisted that missions have been an integral part of their life and work. Any changes in the missionary program may throw light on basic changes in the ideas of the church.

The most important study ever made of American foreign missions was made during the depression of the 1930's. The decrease in giving for foreign missions had begun before the depression began. The sharp downward trend brought some Baptist laymen together to talk over the severe cuts necessary for retrenchment. The Laymen's Foreign Missions Inquiry, with seven denominations participating, was organized in 1930. The first year was given to fact-finding by twenty-seven specialists under the direction of the Institute of Social and Religious Research. The fact finders' reports are known as the *Supplementary Series to Re-Thinking Missions*[23] (covering India, Burma,

---

[22] An illustration is seen in the difference in the fate of the International Council of Religious Education in comparison with the Religious Education Association.

[23] New York: Harper & Brothers. 1933

China, and Japan), Volumes IV, V, VI, and VII. Volumes I, II, and III of the Supplementary Series give the regional reports of the Commission of Appraisal. The Commission made a one-volume report for general circulation in *Re-Thinking Missions.*[24]

The Boards of the seven denominations were called together November 18 and 19, 1932, for a report and discussion. The report was made by "a lay group from inside the churches but outside traditional management of the missionary enterprise." In view of the way in which needed changes in attitudes and methods of mission work were faced, and in view of the frank recognition of the necessity of greater appreciation of the meritorious aspects of religions and cultures other than our own, the report attracted much newspaper comment.

It soon became clear that the missionary boards were not taking up the report "eagerly." In March 1934 the National Committee for the Presentation of the Laymen's Foreign Missions Inquiry reorganized as the National Committee of the Modern Missions Movement. "Rethinking Missions" became a movement, and an institution known as the Modern Missions Movement emerged. Its stated procedure was to praise into existence the forms of missionary work which it could approve. It came to have a paid executive secretary, a research department with a paid personnel, a committee of counsellors, an educational committee, and a biennial institute. It later changed its name to "A Movement for World Christianity" and in January 1937, began a religious quarterly, *World Christianity—A Digest.*

A number of leaders interested in missions think that the trend of modern missions is in the direction indicated by these studies set forth in brief in *Re-Thinking Missions* and represented by the group leading "A Movement for World Christianity." What has the depression done to this supposedly long-time trend? The materials recently prepared are voluminous. The task

[24] Hocking, W. E. Chairman. *Re-thinking Missions.* [A layman's inquiry after one hundred years by the Commission of Appraisal.] New York: Harper & Brothers. 1932

of sensing changes in missions is a very large one. Some study might be made to indicate the attitudes of the mission boards and constituencies to these new proposals. The fact finding reports were not given the study which they deserved. Social scientists might well spend time analyzing the fact finding reports and in studying the more recent reactions to the proposals. A "Movement for World Christianity"[25] is in process and its progress, problems and results might well be under observation and study. It represents an effort to change and crystallize public opinion and to give reorganization and direction to new tendencies within and without the church.[26] The Laymen's Inquiry studied the missionary projects themselves in a most comprehensive fashion; a similarly adequate study of the attitudes that lie behind giving in America is needed. The decline in giving for foreign missions should have careful study. It should be studied by denominations, by regions, by urban and rural differences, by intensive studies of local churches, and by studying the attitudes of the clergy and laity and of different classes of givers.

CHURCH UNION

While church union has been a "program" of the churches, it has implications for changes in the structural organization of the institution itself.

Have sectarian division and lack of cooperation which, according to H. Paul Douglass, were checked before the depression, been definitely affected by the depression? Perhaps some phases of Dr. Douglass' studies should be repeated and give answer to this question.[27]

The appeals for Christian union in sermons and speeches, especially in interdenominational conferences, do not seem to

[25] Ewald, Charles J., Executive Secretary, 140 S. Dearborn St., Chicago; Orville A. Petty, Research Director, 902 Chapel St., New Haven, Conn.

[26] Tibbetts, Norris. *Religious Education.* October 1936, has a good statement on the meaning of The Movement for World Christianity.

[27] See Douglass, H. Paul. *Church Unity Movements in the United States.* New York: Institute of Social and Religious Research. 1934; *Protestant Cooperation in American Cities.* New York: Institute of Social and Religious Research. 1930

have lost their fervor during the depression. In many local fields, however, the task was more difficult during the depression than before the depression. Many ministers have been willing to continue services for "what the people can pay." A number of abandoned churches were opened up by unemployed ministers.[28] While opinions vary it is generally agreed that, for some cause, church unions have not made progress.

CHURCH PHILANTHROPY, RELIEF, AND SOCIAL AND COMMUNITY SERVICE[29]

The depression years have brought to the threshold of the church many problems in the field of philanthropy—aid to its members, aid to its community, and coöperative undertakings in partnership with secular and community agencies. The entire field of philanthropy and relief has been so great a concern and a subject of so much discussion from the point of view of policy and responsibility of the church that it should have special study.

Churches had more to do with relief and aid to the poor in the earlier than in the later days of the depression. Some church workers testify that as the depression wore on they had fewer calls, not because people were in less need, but because their need was so great and so continuous that they themselves realized that only the government could give them adequate aid. Religious institutions and settlements have performed the services of supplying temporary relief. "Invisible relief" has often been in the form of "God's Cupboard." In situations where relief was uncertain or delayed, in families where sickness

[28] Brunner, E. deS., and Lorge, Irving. *Rural Trends in Depression Years.* New York: Columbia University Press. 1937. P. 300

[29] See White, R. Clyde and Mary K. *Research Memorandum on Social Aspects of Relief Policies in the Depression;* and Chapin, F. Stuart and Queen, Stuart A. *Research Memorandum on Social Work in the Depression.* (monographs in this series); see also: *Social Work Yearbook.* New York: Russell Sage Foundation. 1937; Webber, Herman C. (Ed.) *Yearbook of American Churches.* New York: Association Press; Johnson, F. E. (Ed.) *Social Work of the Churches.* Includes bibliography. New York: Federal Council of the Churches of Christ in America. 1930; *Information Service.* Federal Council of the Churches of Christ in America. January 18 1936

existed and where special care was needed, churches, neighborhood houses, and settlements have often given aid.

Only slight investigation reveals the fact that many churches have given much relief during the depression. Complete financial studies cannot be made of this. Correspondence with ministers, however, reveals interesting reactions on the part of individual churches.

The question arose, from time to time, as to what should be the rôle of the church in aiding even its own members. Social workers said that it was legitimate for individual churches "to care for their own." Some newspapers, as for example the *Chicago Tribune,* lent aid on this point. It was thought that this would be a more economical way than public taxation.

Some Protestant church groups advocated Protestant charities to match Catholic and Jewish charities. In the face of well organized Catholic and Jewish relief, and philanthropic societies, Protestant church groups have come to feel the inadequacy of their loosely organized life, at least so far as relief and philanthropies are concerned. In 1934 the Brooklyn Church and Mission Federation put out a booklet called "One in Every Six," in which this position was stated. This document added:

> Our Catholic and Jewish brethren, on the other hand, are better equipped to serve their members in this crisis. Each of these religious bodies has had for many years well organized welfare societies to which the congregations can refer needy members. During the present emergency Catholic and Jewish welfare organizations raise large funds from their own people for use in caring for their own, and in addition obtain appropriations from the general funds raised in city-wide campaigns.
>
> But the crisis caught the Protestant church unprepared and unorganized for this vital Christian service. Consequently, two years ago, the Social Service Department of the Brooklyn Church and Mission Federation was made the clearing house for this Protestant Supplementary Relief and Service Work.

Other large cities found that the fact the Catholic and Jewish groups were organized and the Protestant were not, made for tense situations. The Protestant groups often felt that their welfare institutions were given closer supervision than those of other groups. There developed a tension between the religious groups and the "Social Service Party." In some cases a "givers' strike" attitude resulted. A further result in a number of cases was a rift among Protestant business men themselves, some of whom wanted the community fund to do all relief and philanthropy, while others wanted the church to have a larger share. These movements may have consequences far beyond the financing of philanthropies. It may drive Protestant bodies to find a basis for more complete integration. It may be the basis for communal conflict on a larger scale than we have known. It may be a basis for conflict between church and state. The movement should be studied continuously. Documents and records of meetings and discussions, as well as any newspaper reports of this problem, should be kept. Sometimes the newspapers report quite the reverse of what actually happens in meetings.

One notable effect of the present depression has been the forced realization on the part of the church that relief problems in a major depression are beyond it. Some take the attitude that the church must recover the task of helping the poor, while others say that we are now "beyond the relief stage" and that the task of the church is to speak for a justice which will make relief unnecessary on a major scale. Some writers point to this as the further secularization of the activities of churches. Once the church cared for the poor; now the larger community takes over this task. Other writers point out that aloofness to these problems compels their solution to be in secular terms.[30]

The church groups, especially the ministers, lent themselves to the collection and dissemination of materials revealing the conditions of people in the areas of greatest unemployment. It is said that hearings organized by the clergy in some cities

[30] See Newell, Frederick B. *The City Challenges the Church.* New York: Home Missions Council. 105 E. 22nd St. 1937. P. 87

may have stimulated public opinion in demanding action in bringing relief.[31]

In all probability, separate approaches for the Catholic and Protestant churches will have to be made to study this topic. The effect of the depression has no doubt been noticeable in the inner organization of the Catholic church in terms of dependence of poorer parishes on wealthier ones, in terms of the administration by clergy or laymen of the funds of the parish. As it became more difficult to secure funds, in some parishes in Montreal the priests became willing for the laymen to share responsibilities and to keep the books. Furthermore many local Catholic school boards in Canada, for example, had to appeal to the provincial government for aid during these hard times, enabling the province to acquire certain controls over these Catholic schools in return for this aid.[32]

A unique and much publicized undertaking is the Church Security Program of the Church of Jesus Christ of Latter Day Saints. It was outlined in a radio address by President Henry D. Moyle on September 6, 1936. Pointing out that the temporal welfare of its people had always been a major concern of the church, the speaker explained the organizational division of the church which enables each "ward" to care for the needs of its members and, when such needs exceed the capacities of local resources, the ward may turn to higher units for assistance. "Thus the entire resources of the church are available for the social security of its people," the speaker explained.

Auxiliary relief organizations are created in each ward, such as a woman's relief society, whose primary duty is to assist the bishop in taking care of the social needs of the families. Whereas prior to 1930 this machinery was carried forward primarily to aid the aged and dependent, in recent years the Mormon church

[31] Holt, Arthur E. "An Urban Famine." Mimeographed report of hearings on file at the Chicago Theological Seminary

[32] See Appendix C

has endeavored to care not only for its greater mass of unemployed, but to attack the basic problems of unemployment among its people. The aim is to work with the family, President Moyle pointed out, endeavoring to establish the family as a self-sustaining and supporting unit. Labor surveys made by the church, accumulation of food, fuel, and clothing, cooperative projects, employment agencies, colonization projects, canning, recreational units, and many other features are included in the program.

President Moyle stated: "It is not and has not been the purpose of the social security program of our church to duplicate the work of any municipal, state or federal relief agency, but rather to supplement their work and prepare to minimize the necessity therefor."

Opinions about the real scope and success of the program differ. Although the Mormon church has many unique characteristics, the program should interest research workers seeking to study the rôle of the church in general, in meeting the problems raised by the depression.

INSTITUTIONAL CHURCHES AND NEIGHBORHOOD HOUSES

Churches have been pulled in two main directions so far as institutional church and neighborhood house work is concerned. They have felt the urgency to preserve their own church membership and they have felt the appeal to help those in distress. Even before the depression church leaders were asking how their resources should be distributed between these two major aspects of church work. In which direction did the depression push denominational groups? Even if church groups would have continued in such work before the depression, their efforts would have been overshadowed by the numerous groups supported by government funds. Does the fact that the government has carried on community and recreational work reveal to church groups the community-wide nature of such work as against its more ecclesiastical nature? Are church groups using these government workers with the attitude that the work will of necessity be turned back to them eventually? Do some church people refuse to use them because of fear of entangling alliances of church and state?

With the government and the community at large doing much recreational and community work this activity has been lost to church control. What effect will this have upon the structure and program of churches? Does the use of WPA resources change the basic attitudes of those who run neighborhood houses, or is the conformity with community fund requirements formal and looked upon as "necessary in order to secure funds?"

To what extent did a shift occur during the depression in institutional church and neighborhood house work to make them "thought centers," instead of places of recreation, sources of relief, or institutions with clubs and classes for children? This was a sort of second stage of the depression, the first being the relief emphasis. Many discussion groups and forums were held, resulting in a shift that emphasized the importance of an adult education program.

A study showing cooperation of churches and public agencies could be made on the basis of the study of selected churches. There are a number of interesting cases of this type, of which the Riverside Church in New York City, for example, is one.[33]

A definite project for study would be the problems arising over the distribution of community funds to Protestant neighborhood houses, and to Protestant charities. A financial study of the amounts going into regular church work in comparison with the amounts going into "institutional" churches and neighborhood houses for the country as a whole and by principal cities might well be made. A preliminary examination of such funds in Chicago (Table VIII) shows that the "institutional" work suf-

[33] See the material in the introductory section of this chapter

fered less of a financial decrease, proportionately, than the churches. Moreover, gifts for churches in the Methodist Episcopal, Congregational and Presbyterian of the U.S.A. were definitely less in 1935 than in 1932, while "institutional" work received more support, except in the case of the Presbyterian U.S.A.

TABLE VIII

PERCENTAGE CHANGES IN CHURCH EXPENSES AND IN EXPENDITURES OF PLACES DOING "INSTITUTIONAL" WORK, FOR SELECTED DENOMINATIONS: METROPOLITAN CHICAGO, 1930 TO 1932 AND 1932 TO 1935[a]

Denomination	Percentage Change			
	1930–1932		1932–1935	
	Churches	Inst'l Work	Churches	Inst'l Work
Methodist Episcopal	−20	−20	−22	+8
Cong'l and Presbyterian U.S.A.[b]	−32	−27	−10	−4
M.E., Cong'l and Presby. U.S.A.	−28	−25	−14	−1
Congregational only	−26	−15	−18	+8
Presbyterian only	−35	−31	− 5	−8
Protestant Episcopal	−23	−23	—	+7
M.E., Cong'l, Presby. and Prot. Episcopal	−27	−25	—	+ .5

[a] Prepared for the author by Dr. Gilbert K. Robinson. It is not easy to prepare such materials since lines of work are not sharply drawn in religious institutions

[b] Including joint enterprises

For the Methodist Episcopal, Congregational and Presbyterian U.S.A., the decrease 1930-1935 was 38 per cent for church expenses and only 26 per cent in expenditures for places carrying on "institutional" work.

In 1935 Mr. Ralph Cummins made a study of what had happened to the Presbyterian neighborhood houses during the depression. The Presbyterian neighborhood houses are widely distributed in the cities of the United States. Their grade of work is usually above the average for such work; otherwise they present a fairly typical picture of what goes on in similar institutions. He sought to answer the question "How have the depression years affected the program and work of neighborhood houses?" He found that in the early years of the depression the houses were overburdened with relief needs, and that during the depression there has been a great increase in attendance and program. Part of this increase has been due to the use of government workers. The budgets of the houses exclusive of government aid were greatly reduced, averaging about 50 per cent.[34]

CITY SOCIETIES

It is clear that the city societies of the large cities of America have exerted very great influence in home mission work and on the work of many individual churches.

While New York illustrations are said to be non-typical, especially by Midwesterners, they do reveal processes toward which others may be moving. Dr. Frederick B. Newell, executive secretary, New York City Society, Methodist Episcopal Church, makes the generalization that the depression period has been a "devastating" one for city organizations such as his own.[35] It is his contention that the city society has been making changes for the last decade but that the processes of change have been greatly speeded up during the depression. There is less stress on foreign language churches, less emphasis upon evangelism, parish visiting, and home prayer meetings. Much greater emphasis has come in the care of children.[36] One of the major tasks of the city society has been the administration of funds. The decrease of funds of the Methodist City Society of New York has been very great. To quote Dr. Newell:

> Our own receipts in New York City, not including Brooklyn, Staten Island, or Queens, from our Board of Home Missions in the year 1921 for current maintenance of missionary work was $170,023.34. A large church extension appropriation was received in addition to this. By 1930, the year in which I became the Secretary of the Society, this amount had been reduced to $92,931.26. In 1935, which was the low point of our World Service income, the amount had been further reduced to $29,432.90. . . . It is probable that my observations of the result of

[34] *Neighborhood Houses in a Period of Depression.* New York: Board of National Missions. 156 Fifth Ave.

[35] "The City Societies." *The City Challenges the Church.* New York: Home Missions Council. 1937. Pp. 81ff.

[36] *Ibid.* P. 82

this great reduction may not be equally true of all denominations but it would seem, as far as the Methodists are concerned, that the reduction resulted in two evils. In the first place, the temptation to allow the missionary appropriation to become very thinly spread was almost universal. In the second place, it became impossible to distinguish the missionary grants in some cases from sustentation grants, which in our church come under a different heading and are supplied from a different source. The general result of this was that the missionary program of the church as conducted and supervised by City Societies ceased to have outstanding centers which attracted the attention and the gifts of the denomination. Likewise, the work of these centers in many cases was diminished to the point where it no longer could approach its work from an experimental and laboratory viewpoint but rather from the viewpoint of mere subsistence.[37]

Dr. Newell points out that in many communities these weakened institutions of the various denominations are in competition with each other and that there is need for discovering the ways in which all the resources may be brought to bear upon the welfare of the local community.

A major change in church administration seems to be taking place, says Dr. Newell, in that the city society is compelled to raise its own money and thereby to have a spirit of independence and even parochialism in relation to the national and international work and organization.[38]

The New York City Society of the Methodist Episcopal Church has taken the position that it will cooperate rather than compete with the government alphabet agencies. Dr. Newell's statement is so significant for possible changes in the relationship of church and state, that it is quoted at length.

In the second and third years, however, of the Roosevelt administration when an appropriation of over $4,000,000,000 was made to be used further to cope with the unemployment and depression situation, a new phase of competition faced the religious forces. It seemed that the leaders of many of these alphabet projects had become convinced that you could not cure the evils of great cities by legalism alone but that education should be used also. Our first experience in New York was when we

[37] *Ibid.* P. 83
[38] *Ibid.* P. 84

were approached by the Works Progress Administration with the suggestion that, through their relationship with the Crime Prevention Bureau, educational, artistic, social and gymnastic classes should be opened in our centers to be staffed by their workers. Many of our churches were reluctant to consider the overture at all. Some of them were so impoverished financially that the additional expense of heat and light could not be borne. Certain denominations have taken a very definite stand that they do not desire to cooperate with this new form of social education. Our own Methodist Society in New York has perhaps been as advanced as any in pleading for a cooperative arrangement whereby these projects and our churches could work together. Some of our experiments in this line have been most dismal failures. After two months of occupancy in one of our centers the breakage of property, the disrespect of the workers for our religious viewpoint, the lack of educational and cultural qualification of the workers, the inability to develop a motive for their work or an end for their achievement, made us so disheartened that we terminated the relationship almost instantaneously. In other centers we have been more successful and in one, particularly, where we have an excellent excutive with an educational viewpoint and an understanding of the social needs of the community, we have had most delightful cooperation and the two groups have worked together until, at present, it is difficult to distinguish which workers are government workers and which are supplied by the church. We have even now gone beyond this point to the place where we have encouraged the Works Progress Administration to open projects with us. Thus we opened a Nursery School for Negro children last winter. Another nursery school and kindergarten in a white neighborhood has proved to be a very successful enterprise likewise. We realize fully that there is a deep disagreement as to whether the church should cooperate or compete. We realize fully that there is a question of the ultimate regimentation of the church by the government were this relationship to become too close. We realize fully that the traditional belief of Protestantism as to the transformation of a human being through the power and presence of God is difficult to keep foremost in such a cooperative program. And yet we believe that we have made our choice wisely and that daily we are making progress in this new direction which we have chosen. . . . It might be wise to set forth somewhat as an illustration the outcome of the study of the Metropolitan Federation of Daily Vacation Bible Schools in New York regarding this subject. For fourteen years, from 1920 to 1933 inclusive, the average attendance at Daily Vacation Bible Schools in the metropolitan area increased. From 1934 to 1936 inclusive it has decreased. From 1920 to 1933 the average attendance at these schools either increased or was stationary. From 1933 to 1936 it has decreased every year. This is in spite of the fact that in 1936 we had more schools and raised more funds with which to support them. So acute is the problem that it became desirable to study the reasons for this set of figures. A special committee was appointed and in the beginning of its study it found that practically every school reported certain public agencies which had entered into competition. These public agencies conducted the following educational and play opportunities: playgrounds, swimming pools, all-day excursions to parks and museums, dramatics in public summer schools, street games, craft work, day camps, community singing for children, community dancing for children, free lunches, street showers.

The Board of Education of our city alone employed 1500 regular staff workers and 1000 emergency relief workers in the summer activities of its play schools, camps, etc. last summer. Practically every Daily Vacation Bible School which was examined cited the reason for its diminishing attendance as the competition of these outside public agencies. Moreover these public agencies were able to plan their work from a juvenile delinquency map rather than the center which happened to be owned in a certain locality. Furthermore they were staffed adequately and given sufficient materials with which to work.

Recently listening to one of the public school-teacher's reports, I heard the following aims for their camp and vacation schools set forth: To develop—1. Good mental health; 2. Physical health and personal appearance. 3. Proper environment. 4. Group consciousness and responsibility; 5. Proper use of leisure time; 6. A stabilized emotional tone; 7. The discovery of hidden talents. 8. Self-respect. 9. Understanding of complex relationships. 10. A desire for a cultural heritage.[39]

Studies should be made to see to what extent these New York changes are typical of the changes in other large cities.

THE CHURCH AND COOPERATIVES

There has been a development in teaching and practice in "Christian Cooperatives" during the depression—a development in which the churches have played a large part and which has comprised an important phase of church activity in many instances. Following upon our preceding discussion of secularization, it might be well said that in these cooperatives there is a process that is the reverse of secularization—a process in which the church's influence and many of its principles are extended

[39] *The City Challenges the Church.* Pp. 87-89. (See note 30, p. 105)

back into the world of business and trade. Churches themselves however, do not seem to be organizing many cooperatives.

Discussion of the growth of the cooperative movement in its more secular forms during the depression is outside of the scope of this monograph.[40] There has been an effort on the part of a number of church leaders to interpret cooperatives as the "Christian economic order." This movement was given acceleration by the Japanese leader, Toyohiko Kagawa, who visited the United States in 1936. In some quarters an effort was made to form a "Kingdom of God Fellowship" on the basis of the impetus given by Kagawa.

Under the inspiration and counsel of Toyohiko Kagawa's farewell messages at Lake Geneva, June 27-30, 1936 and organization known as The Christian Cooperative Fellowship in North-American was formed. The statement of organization and purpose from a bulletin announcing the movement is:

> This vast concentration of economic and consequent political power in the hands of the owning few constitutes a deadly peril. It makes for growing tension and conflict at home. It produces class war, mounting armaments and growing menace of world conflict abroad. The time has come when all people of good will must help to replace a narrow and selfish individualism by the cooperative way of life.

This organization has in it a number of people interested in religion and the cooperatives but it is only a meager indication of the interest on the part of church people in making religion more vital in the realm of economics. Some writers and speakers are taking the position that the next great aspect of life which needs to be thought through by church people is in this realm of economics. Thus a bishop writes:

> As men's thoughts have shifted from political toward economic considerations, we are developing what might be called an "economic-mindedness." This has penetrated the church and stabbed it wide awake

[40] See Vaile, Roland S. *Research Memorandum on Social Aspects of Consumption in the Depression.* (monograph in this series)

to the fact that "religion and economics are not two things but two sides of one thing—the inside and the outside."[41]

The Christian Century has sought and published several statements on the meaning of cooperatives for religious groups as, for example. the articles by Horace M. Kallen on the meaning and philosophy of cooperatives.

Business men in churches often taken positions at opposite poles on the place of cooperatives. Some good churchmen in business look upon cooperatives as the entering wedge of communism. Some simply see a competitor to their business. Some churchmen in business welcome the cooperatives as more than an economic form and see in it the basis for a reorganization of our economic life on a more humanitarian and Christian foundation. The following passage is from an address of Mr. Edward A. Filene, a prominent business man in Boston, delivered before the synod of New York of the Presbyterian Church in the U.S.A., in Brooklyn, New York, October 21, 1936.[42]

> The cooperative movement, to be sure, is basically economic, as was the family and other institutions which have made it possible for man to realize so many of his spiritual ideals. But it is more than economic. It is charged with aspiration and with idealism. It is warmly, humanly passionate; and it is demonstrating day by day that there is more real satisfaction and more business success in working together for the common good than there ever could be in a free-for-all struggle on the part of everybody to get ahead of everybody else. And many churches, I am glad to say, of many faiths and creeds, are already helping to organize such cooperation.

SURVEY OF LOCAL CHURCHES

In the study of the program and activities of the church, perhaps more than in the case of any of the other problems proposed, investigation must be made of individual local churches.

---

[41] Personal correspondence

[42] Quoted almost in full in *Information Service.* New York: Department of Research and Education. Federal Council of Churches of Christ in America. Vol. XV, No. 35

Regional differences as discussed in Appendix A must be examined. Time case studies of local churches should permit reconstruction of the programs and activities for the period prior to, as well as during, the depression and recovery phases of the business cycle. Guide questions and schedules might be constructed for broader studies of this problem on the basis of experience gained from individual local surveys. For a further discusson of local church survey methods the reader is referred to Appendix B.

Appendix A

Regional and Rural Variations

IT IS NOT justifiable to think that we have secured the whole picture of increase or decrease in church membership, or in church finance by a study of the national figures. Further light may be thrown upon the membership and financial increase and decrease by an analysis on the basis of the regions in which losses and gains occur.[1]

Any studies which attempt to generalize on the entire country so far as the changes in message during the depression is concerned have very definite difficulties to overcome. The student of religion in America is forced to recognize the very great differences in the content of sermon materials and in church literature in the regions of the country. While the regional variations here described are in terms of members and finances they should be kept in mind when plans are made for the study of the changes in message.[2]

The analysis on the basis of regions becomes more important when we know the social, cultural, and economic conditions which are present in the regions. A complete study of these regional variations might be revealing regarding the relation of religion to these various conditioning factors.

The total increase or decrease of a single denomination may

---

[1] See on the topic of religion and sectionalism, Maurer, Heinrich H. "Religion and American Sectionalism." *American Journal of Sociology.* 30:408-438. No. 4. January 1925; see also 30:665-682. No. 6. May 1925; and 31:39-57. No. 1. July 1925; 31:485-506. No. 4. January 1926; also Douglass, H. Paul, and Brunner, Edmund deS. *The Protestant Church as a Social Institution.* New York: Harper & Brothers. 1935. P. 238

[2] See Chapter V, "The Message."

help to get at the regional differences to the extent that the denomination is a regional one. Much more light may be thrown upon the fate of the denomination during the depression by a regional and typical situation study of the particular denomination. Within a denomination there may be significant local differences.

The commonly acceptable "principle" that denominations which are dominant in a community attract disproportionately large numbers of adherents may have special application during depression times. In Chicago and Illinois studies made by the Department of Research and Survey of the Chicago Theological Seminary and the Chicago Congregational Union, this "principle" had been clearly seen.[3] The principal regional differences which we find are related to long time processes of change which are speeded up by the depression. At least, the presence of these major characteristics has become better known to church officers and administrators during the depression. These long term trends in membership are related to the strata of the population in which a church group finds itself and the accompanying birth rate of that group, their ability to penetrate other groups, and the type of service in relationship to the cultural patterns which exist in the area.

Some brief sketches from various regions indicate that a complete study of the characteristic regions of the country and the relationship of church experiences to those factors would be valuable. In the first place, we need to keep in mind the regional variations as revealed in the Federal Census of Religious Bodies and analyzed by C. Luther Fry in *The U. S. Looks at Its Churches,* and to recognize the regional nature of many denominations. A similar study should be made of the new Census of Religious Bodies. An effort should be made to have a much more comprehensive picture of the cultural and economic regions within the U. S. than we have ever had.

[3] Studies on file in the Chicago Theological Seminary

The regional differences and differences in church life may be illustrated within a state such as Illinois. Many writers would readily speak of state averages but one cannot use the total figures of even a so-called northern state without knowing that the general averaging process may eliminate significant variations.

The state of Illinois has within it distinct regions both industrially and culturally speaking. The great metropolitan area of Chicago gives a large territory of urban life. Heavy dairying counties are found in northeastern Illinois. South of Chicago and in the eastern section of Illinois is the cash corn region. To the west and south central parts are found mixed farming and animal husbandry. The southern fourth of Illinois where peach and apple orchards abound is still different, with a different soil and more hills. Both coal and oil are found in Illinois and have their implications for the distribution of religion.

Regions within the state of Illinois may be seen in terms of health as illustrated by the map from the Illinois Regional Planning Association, with data from the Illinois Department of Health, in which deaths for three sections of the state from infant mortality, tuberculosis and typhoid fever are shown. In 1928 to 1932 in the northern part of the state the average infant mortality rate was 55.9; in the central part of the state the rate was 59.1; in the southern part of the state the rate was 72.9. The death rate in 1933 from tuberculosis in the northern part of the state was 38.2 per 100,000; in the central part 43.0, and in the southern part 57.3. The death rate in 1933 from typhoid fever in the northern part of the state was 0.6 per 100,000; in the central part of the state it was 2.3, while in the southern part of the state it was 5.

The map of the Regional Planning Association which shows the percentage of farms located on concrete, brick, asphalt and macadam roads, reveals the fact that the highest percentage of farms located on such roads is found about the cities and in the northern part of the state, next to the highest in the central part of the state, and the lowest in the southern part of the state.

These more objective data are indicative of the cultural and religious differences which are not so easily pictured. A study of church membership with a knowledge of the characteristics of various groups reveals the fact that cultural and religious differences correspond roughly with the distribution of these other data.

The mapping of the distribution of church membership in Illinois (see accompanying figures) reveals the concentration of the various religious denominations in Illinois by areas.[4] This study of the distribution of the church members of various denominations in Illinois by counties reveals the fact that Catholic churches are most heavily concentrated in the great urban centers, but that there are 38 counties out of 102 counties in Illinois in which from 20 to 50 per cent of the total church population is Catholic. There are six counties in the state of Illinois in which over 50 per cent of the total church membership is Catholic.

The Missouri Synod Lutheran Church has a concentration in the northern and another in the central part of the state. The Augustana Synod Lutheran is concentrated in the northern part of the state. This is the area of the heavy Swedish migrations into Illinois. There are eight northern counties in the state of Illinois where the Augustana Synod Lutheran group constitutes from 10 to 20 per cent of the total church population.

The Northern Baptists are most heavily concentrated in the central part of the state while the Southern Bapists are, as we would expect, strongest in the southern part of the state. There is one county in which they constitute over 50 per cent of the total church population and there are nine counties in which

[4] *Census of Religious Bodies*. U. S. Bureau of the Census. 1926. It is recognized that there is some error in these charts because of the differences in requirements for church membership by different denominations. (Base maps used by permission of the American Map Company)

RATIO OF ROMAN CATHOLIC CHURCH MEMBERSHIP TO TOTAL CHURCH MEMBERSHIP BY COUNTIES IN ILLINOIS

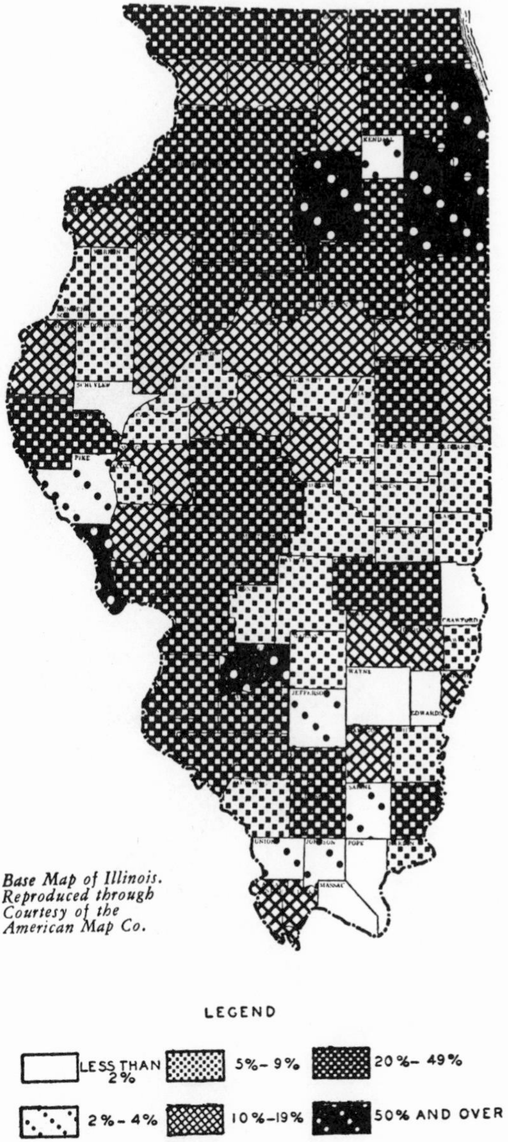

FIGURE 4

RATIO OF METHODIST EPISCOPAL CHURCH MEMBERSHIP TO TOTAL CHURCH MEMBERSHIP BY COUNTIES IN ILLINOIS

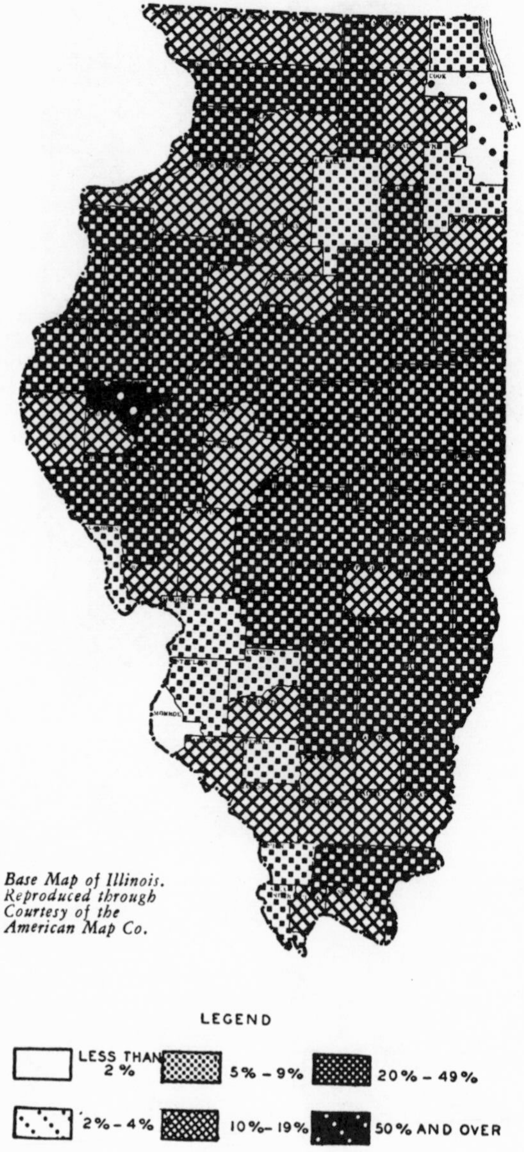

FIGURE 5

RATIO OF PRESBYTERIAN CHURCH MEMBERSHIP TO TOTAL CHURCH MEMBERSHIP, BY COUNTIES IN ILLINOIS

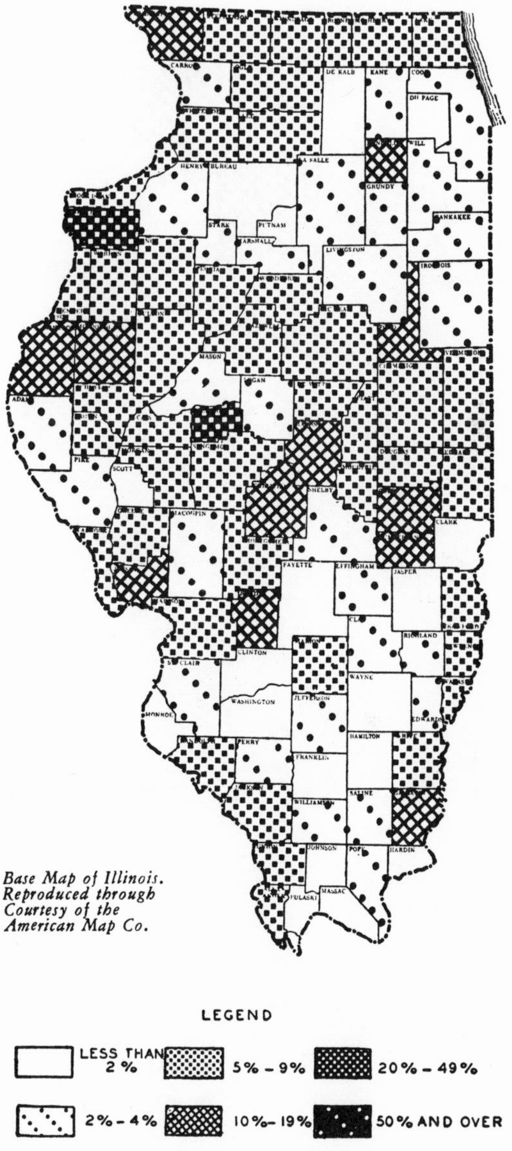

FIGURE 6

RATIO OF CONGREGATIONAL CHURCH MEMBERSHIP TO TOTAL MEMBERSHIP BY COUNTIES IN ILLINOIS

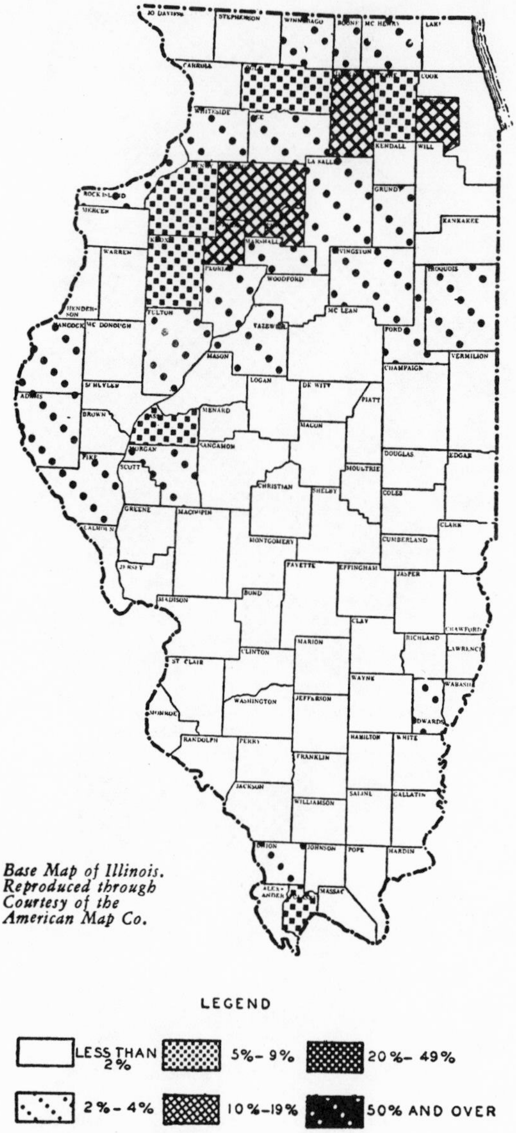

FIGURE 7

RATIO OF DISCIPLES OF CHRIST CHURCH MEMBERSHIP TO TOTAL CHURCH MEMBERSHIP BY COUNTIES IN ILLINOIS

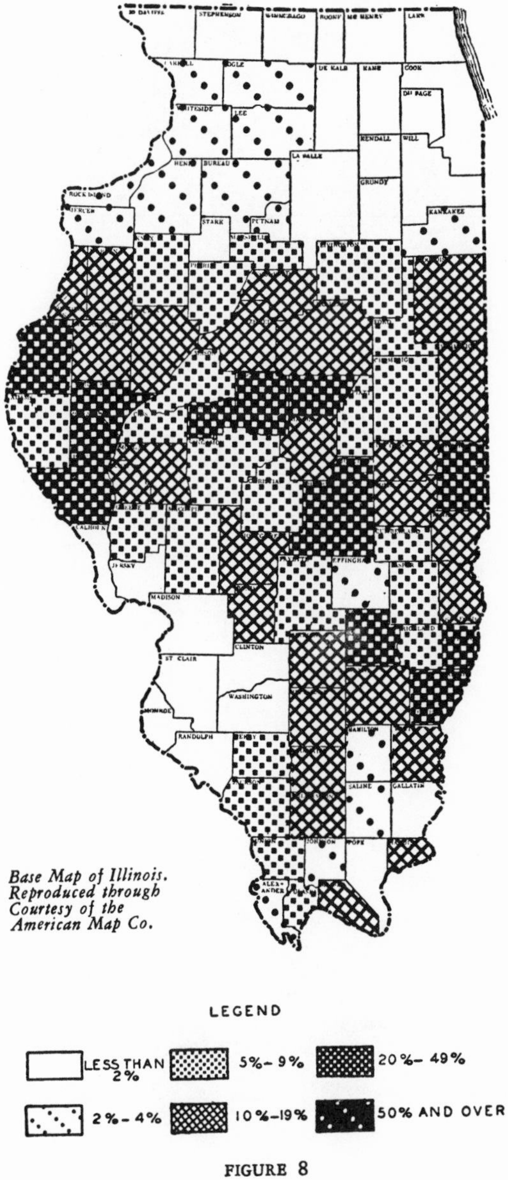

FIGURE 8

RATIO OF LUTHERAN AUGUSTANA SYNOD CHURCH MEMBERSHIP TO TOTAL CHURCH MEMBERSHIP BY COUNTIES IN ILLINOIS

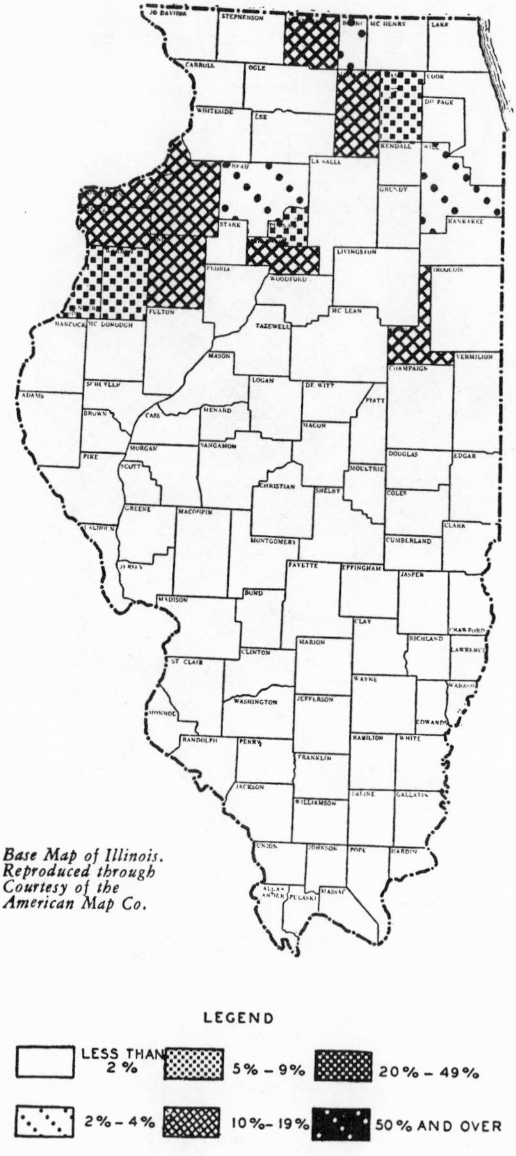

FIGURE 9

RATIO OF NORTHERN BAPTIST CHURCH MEMBERSHIP TO TOTAL CHURCH MEMBERSHIP BY COUNTIES IN ILLINOIS

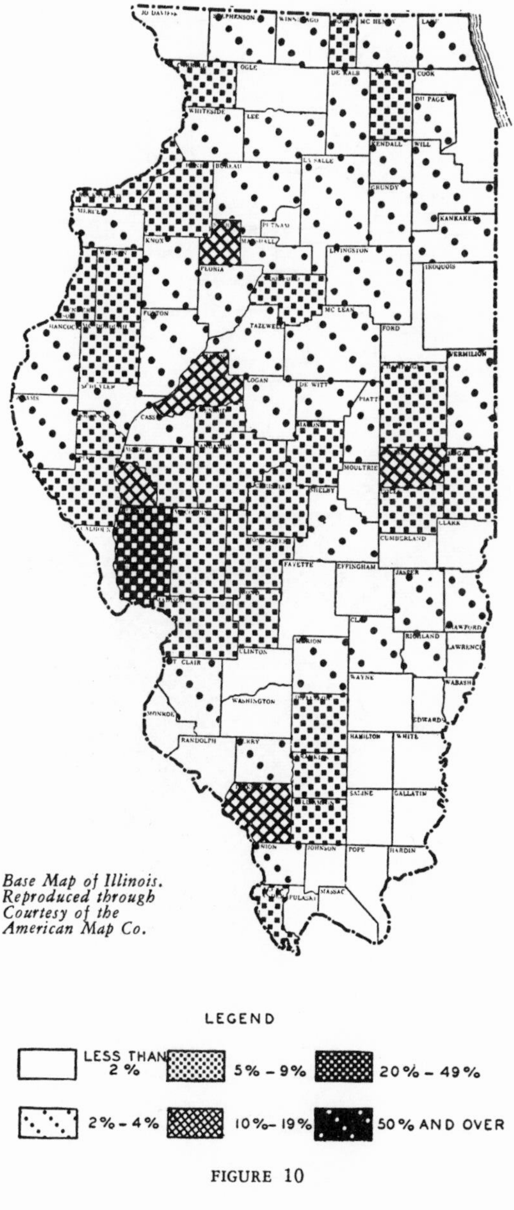

FIGURE 10

RATIO OF SOUTHERN BAPTIST CHURCH MEMBERSHIP TO TOTAL CHURCH MEMBERSHIP BY COUNTIES IN ILLINOIS

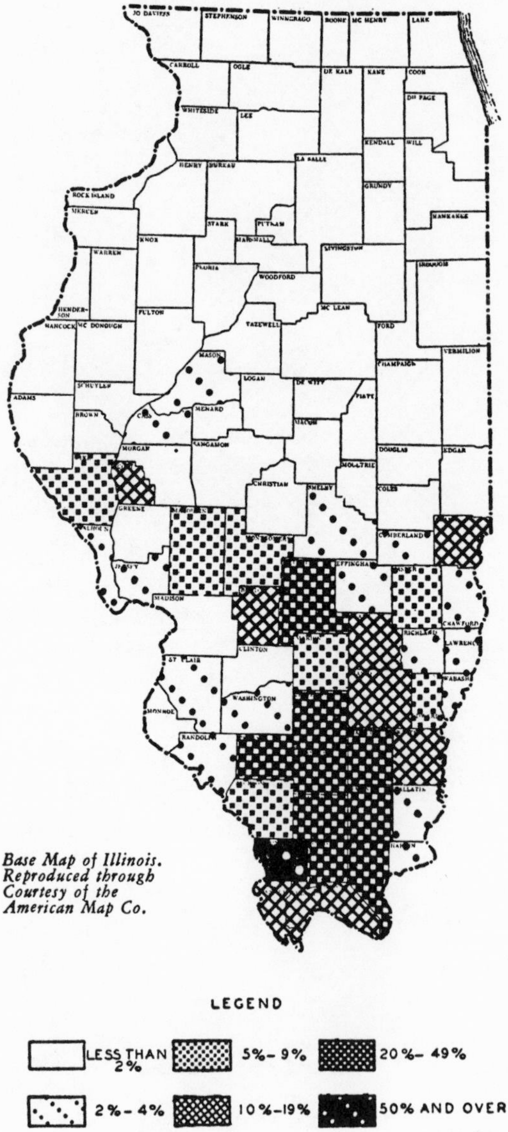

FIGURE 11

their membership constitutes from 20 to 50 per cent of the total church population. All of these nine counties are in the southern part of the state.

The Disciples are most numerous in the central part of the state. The Presbyterians are most heavily concentrated in the central part of the state but a little to the north. They have a more urban concentration than have some of the other groups. A very small percentage of their total state membership is found south of Effingham County. They have had difficulty in maintaining their members in southern and rural parts of Illinois. Some of these areas show definite loss, both in membership and in finances. The Congregationalists are definitely concentrated in the northern part of Illinois and show an interesting relationship to the distribution of the Presbyterians. The center of the Congregational distribution in Illinois is north of that of the Presbyterians. They also have many of their members in urban areas. The churches of the former Christian denomination are most heavily concentrated in Jasper, Crawford, Clay, Richland, Lawrence, and Edwards Counties, across the river and to the north from Vincennes, Indiana. Their churches are very definitely rural. They have suffered losses in number of churches and in membership.

The Methodist Episcopal Church has the most widespread distribution of any denomination in the state. There are 55 counties where the Methodist church membership constitutes from 20 to 50 per cent of the total church membership. Their wide distribution over the nation and over the state gives them a definite advantage where there is movement of members from one locality to another. A Methodist stands a much better chance of finding a church of his own tradition than do members of minority groups.

These studies of concentration of church members of the various denominations in Illinois are significant for the planning of comity relationships among various denominations. They are significant for each denomination when it seeks an answer to the question as to where it shall seek to maintain churches. Each one of the denominations in the state may need to give up certain locations. The accompanying maps indicate that, within Illinois, there is a kind of religious regionalism. Church groups prosper by areas and regions.

A study of the growth of several of the principal British-American denominations reveals the fact that the Methodists have had the largest and the most consistent gains in the state of Illinois. Their life line reveals the fact that, from 1890 to 1930, they have increased 109 per cent as compared with an increase of 98 per cent in the population of the state. The Presbyterian rate of growth in the state of Illinois was greater during the earlier periods, the Census of Religious Bodies indicating a slackening up during the census period from 1916 to 1926. The Disciples likewise had a better growth in earlier decades than they have had in the most recent. Congregational membership of the state had a fairly good increase up to 1890. Since 1910, however, the Congregational growth has been retarded.

A major problem for further study would be the regional and situational variations of the effects of the depression upon churches in various types of urban areas. The new Census of Religious Bodies should provide masses of data showing changes since 1926, but it must be remembered that these data will not reflect the worst of the depression. Even if they did, local studies would still be desirable. In making these local studies, one must be cautious about generalization from one local church or one local community. In any one great urban area, there would be many different situations and reactions. This may account for the fact that priests, ministers, and rabbis with whom the writer has talked, within the same metropolitan area, can have such varied opinions regarding the effects of the depression. General population movements, while they have been slowed down, have been going on. One minister may be on the losing and another on the receiving end of a population movement within an urban area. People tend to universalize from their own immediate experiences and thus one man may feel that the depression has increased church attendance while another blames the depression for the losses which he suffers.

RURAL CHURCHES[5]

While rural-urban differences in many aspects of life are lessening, the contrasts between rural and urban are still very sharp. Since the problems of the rural church in the depression have been very competently discussed by Brunner and Lorge and since the monograph in this series by Dwight Sanderson treats of research needed in the subject, this discussion will be brief and illustrative—not systematic or complete.

In many respects the rural church has presented unique problems during the depression. This arises primarily as a result of the fact that agriculture has been in a depressed state all through the twenties so that the depression, as commonly conceived, was not an incident unique to the early 1930's.[6] For this reason it might be well to attempt to study the effects of the depression upon all of the aspects of the rural church as compared with the urban church. Rural and urban church life from 1920 to 1929 and from 1929 to 1936 might be contrasted with reference to membership and attendance, finance, message and program and activities.

The agricultural depression has not been of equal intensity throughout the country. There were areas, of which the Dakotas are illustrations, where the conditions were much more severe

---

[5] Brunner, Edmund deS. and Lorge, Irving. *Rural Trends in Depression Years.* Chapter XII, Pp. 299-328; and Sanderson, Dwight. *Research Memorandum on Rural Life in the Depression.* (monograph in this series)

[6] See Brunner, Edmund deS. and Kolb, J. H. *Rural Social Trends.* New York: McGraw-Hill Book Co., 1933. Chapter II; see also Report of President's Research Committee. *Recent Social Trends.* New York: McGraw-Hill Book Co. 1933. Vol. I. Pp. 498-501

than elsewhere. Ministers and state secretaries, writing from these areas, say that the depression of the 1930's did not make so much difference. For years in some of these areas churches have been on a mere existence level. The annual fluctuations are sharper than are the depression years. In areas such as Iowa and Illinois, where there were heavy debt obligations and where the taxes were high, the severe years of the depression were relatively more catastrophic. It was in such areas and under such circumstances that many rural ministers had very little cash from their congregations.

It is important to have in mind the financial trend in rural and village churches before the depression in order to sense what struck when the final crisis came. A comprehensive statement by C. Luther Fry made in 1928[7] gives us a basis for understanding an important aspect of this problem:

The amounts of home-mission money distributed each year by Protestant bodies are large. Five denominations alone are known to give an aggregate of more than $5,000,000 each year. This is the interest on a hundred million dollars.

Most of the home-mission monies distributed to churches are given to native-white churches. In the case of the Presbyterians, the amount turned over to native-white churches was $946,000 out of $1,333,000 or more than 70 per cent of the total. In the sample of Protestant Episcopal Churches studied, nearly 90 per cent of the money given as aid went to native-white churches. Home mission grants are, therefore, being used primarily to help native-white rather than Negro, Indian or foreign churches.

The great majority of native-white churches aided are located in rural areas. Out of 2,121 native white Presbyterian churches, 1,700 or four-fifths were so located. For the Protestant Episcopal churches studied this proportion was 60 per cent and for the Baptist it was over 70 per cent.

The fact that by far the largest group of churches receiving aid are native-white churches in rural areas becomes doubly important when it is remembered that a large proportion of the rural churches aided, particularly those in villages, are in communities in which several other Protestant churches are located. Analysis of 343 aided churches, located

[7] *Home Mission Aid.* New York: Institute of Social and Religious Research. 1928. P. 24

in small villages of 1,000 population or less, revealed that 205 or nearly 60 per cent of them were in places that had at least one other Protestant church.

The financial condition of rural churches was influenced not alone by the decline of income of the rural communities, but also by the decline in contributions to rural and village churches from the home missionary societies. This threw a burden on these churches when the depression struck. A very large number of rural churches were not on a self-supporting basis before the impact of the depression. The home missionary societies reduced their gifts but there was no arrangement whereby adequate counsel could be given for the reorganization of village and rural church life. The economic base for the older denominations with their standard of living was not there. In many instances slow decline by all the churches and eventually death on the part of some took place, rather than a vigorous reorganization of the religious life. These conditions on the part of the older denominations made possible the entrance and advance of the more highly emotionalized groups.

The benevolence giving of both village and open-country churches dropped very sharply at the depth of the depression. The same general picture is maintained here with reference to the parts of the budget which were cut during the depression.[8]

> . . . As the depression grew more severe the problem of survival, especially for the open-country churches, grew more acute; hence there was less money for the benevolence work of the denominations. The salary of the pastor and bills for coal and light had to be given first consideration. Of the total per member gifts in the village churches, therefore, only $1.79 went for missionary and benevolent purposes. This was a decline of practically one-half from 1930 and of more than two-thirds as compared with 1924. In the open-country churches, the amount was $1.13, a drop proportionately almost, but not quite, as large as in the village churches.
>
> This decline set in sometime after 1924. The drop to 1930 was quite severe; and was clearly associated, in part, with declining interest in

[8] See Chapter II, "Church Finances."

missionary activities abroad and impatience with the competitive use of benevolence funds at home in grants-in-aid. The subsequent decline was more influenced by the depression than by other considerations.[9]

The only accurate figures available on rural church attendance over a period are those of Brunner and Lorge. ". . . The test of attendance is" they say, "probably the fairest index of interest in the activities of the church. The record on this point shows a decided falling off on the part of resident members."[10]

A number of problems appear to be of special importance among the rural churches and deserve special study. One such problem is the development of community churches. According to a report of Sneed and Ensminger of the rural church in Missouri, union movements appear to have been intensified there.

> Churches have been established on the average for 50 years while more than 8 per cent of the churches reported have been established since 1923. Of the churches established since 1925 approximately one-half were of united types. Economic conditions have at least temporarily intensified union movements of one type or another. Individual expressions in regard to the need for a community church were about evenly divided pro and con.[11]

On the other hand a study made by Mr. Ralph Cummins in Illinois seemed to indicate a lack of interest in union movements.[12]

The essence of Mr. Cummins' findings are:

> The number of overchurched small towns in Illinois, I believe, is very large. Many beautiful buildings were erected in these towns, mostly prior to 1920, and at a time when agriculture and mining were in a flourishing state. Now, with a declining population in many of these towns (particularly in the mining towns where the losses have been most severe) there is no outlook that the communities will be able to support these religious institutions in such large numbers in a proper way. It

---

[9] Brunner and Lorge. *Op. cit.* P. 309

[10] *Ibid.* P. 302

[11] Sneed, Melvin W., and Ensminger, Douglas. *The Rural Church in Missouri.* Research Bulletin 225. Columbia: University of Missouri. 1935. P. 70

[12] From MS of his studies on file in the offices of the Social Ethics Department of the Chicago Theological Seminary.

is not uncommon to find a town of 1,000 people with four or five churches and but one resident minister.

I saw almost no signs of the development of any interest in federation or union of churches during the depression.

Many survived through the doing away with a "regular preacher." Sunday school under lay leadership was continued, an occasional preaching service might be held when the preacher was paid a small honorarium. If the church had a "manse" it would be rented to some one in town if possible. I found many "manses" not used by preachers.

Some churches were able to secure ministers who were without jobs through offering them the free use of a manse and very little salary with the minister attempting to seek out an existence by some other means. I could point to a number of Presbyterian churches in Illinois where the salary had been from $400 to $600 per year and use of manse.

An attempt was often made to "yoke fields" so that a minister might have two or more charges which could provide him a living. Many difficulties were encountered in trying to bring this about such as where the minister would live, the hours of service, the amount each church was to pay, etc. Small towns close to one another tended to be great rivals with notable social cleavages between people of the same denomination in the two towns.

The depression, therefore, did not develop a direct attack upon the matter of Protestant over-churching as a real problem. Rather it developed an interest on the part of each church to "survive in spite of everything," using different methods of surviving. In our Presbyterian group the "yoking of fields" made some headway.

Another problem that may be of greater significance among the rural than the urban churches was the composition of the ministry. It is reported by Sneed and Ensminger that there has been a greater use of seminary students, part time ministers and ministers with other supplementary occupations, during the depression. The study of Mr. Cummins agrees with this.

Brunner and Lorge report an improvement in the education of the clergy in the rural areas studied. They state the reasons for the improvement:

The reasons for this improvement are not hard to find. The depression has made more trained men available to the churches, as well as in the public schools. City churches have had to release assistant pastors or directors of religious education. Overhead agencies of the denominations have been forced to reduce staff. The slow but sure decline in the number of churches especially in the open country, has reduced the number of available jobs. The efforts of the denominations to train men, as described above, are beginning to bear fruit, especially since fewer city jobs have been available to men so trained, whose better records in their parishes under normal conditions would have resulted in calling a number of them to urban parishes.[13]

A problem which is uniquely an open-country church problem, is the possible villageward trend in rural church membership. The Missouri studies made by Sneed and Ensminger indicate that this has occurred. The significance of such movement lies in the possible fact that a large village or small town church might conceivably afford better religious services and facilities than a number of small scattered and isolated churches. This problem then requires study from three aspects: (1) has there been a villageward movement of rural church members, and (2) how, if at all, does the village or town church differ from the open-country church, and (3) how does the defection of the presumably more vigorous farm people from the rural church affect the people who do not feel at home in the village churches or who do not have sufficient resources to provide adequate services in the open country?

The depression growth of emotional sects like the Nazarene and Pentecostal groups in some rural areas is said to be pronounced. These advances seem unevenly distributed. The Nazarenes around Danville, Illinois, have made definite advances. In many instances they have bought churches from other denominations.

> Time and time again [reports Ralph Cummins[14]] one would hear that the Nazarenes were the only live group in town. In several places their ministers were said to be receiving the largest salaries of any ministers in the community and their church services well attended. Generally speaking 'life' and 'real enthusiasm' were attributed to this group. At least four new Nazarene churches had been organized or built in this Danville region since 1930. Unquestionably they were the only

[13] Brunner and Lorge. *Op. cit.* P. 318

[14] Unpublished MS.

religious group which appeared to be making real progress. Many of the old line denominational groups were pretty 'dead'."

According to Brunner and Lorge there are regional variations in the successes of the "emotional sects."

. . . In the Far West, the increase of candidates for the ministry has been startling. It is perhaps related to the increased interest in religion, as shown by the gain in the proportion of the population in church reported above. It is also clearly an indication of the success of such special groups as the Four-Square Gospel and other emotional sects to gain recruits for starting new churches of such sects, which are stronger on the Pacific coast then elsewhere.

The clash over philosophies of the function of the church and over the use of government paid workers is found in village and rural situations as it is also found in urban areas. Just how extensive these problems are is not known but observation and the materials available would lead one to judge that they form the basis of many community conflicts in many states.[15]

In order to get an adequate picture of the effect of the depression upon churches one would have to seek out the many variations and build classifications of reactions on the basis of many concrete studies.[16]

---

[15] See Brunner and Lorge. *Op. cit.* Pp. 314-315

[16] For a study in method, see Fry, C. Luther. *Diagnosing the Rural Church.* Garden City: Doubleday, Doran & Co. 1924

See, for basic bibliography on the rural church and many valuable suggestions for research, "Research in Rural Institutions." New York: *Social Science Research Council Bulletin No. 18.* 1933. Pp. 73-112

Appendix B

Notes on the Study of the Local Church in the Depression

A METHODOLOGY for studying the local church in the depression may well involve the use of all the methods of the social sciences. The big task is that of adaptation to a special content. Until much more groundwork is done, the more simple statistical procedures will need to be used. But what is needed most of all at the present time is insight into what the problems are. The general pictures need to be sharpened up. One of the greatest fields for significant hypotheses, however, may be in the realm of exceptions to the general rules. Therefore, emphasis should be placed on area and situational variations in institutional reactions, with exploratory studies into the realm of changes in attitudes and in the traditional reactions which people are making to the institutionalized forms of religion.

In earlier chapters it was suggested that a general picture of membership and attendance and of finance be secured. Appendix A points out the necessity for analysis on the basis of regions. Concrete suggestions are brought together in this appendix for the study of the local church and the individual church member.

A number of people make the assumption that the effects of the depression are so varied that no generalization can be made. As a professor of social ethics states it:

I doubt whether the effects that appear on the surface are sufficiently consistent to enable anyone to judge by them. For example in the Second

Church in ——— where I served during the first four and one half years of the depression, the effects were:

1. The reduction by ½ of the church's income per year.
2. The shrinking of the congregation by about ⅓.
3. The decline of the Sunday-school.
4. The development in the congregation of great intellectual confusion.
5. The extension of religious apathy through the parish.

On the other hand, in the First Church in ——— where ——— ——— was and is pastor, these effects were not seen. The income, while reduced, remained nearly at its previous level. The congregations increased. The Sunday-school spilled over its equipment. No intellectual confusion was to be marked. Religious enthusiasm seemed to increase.

Now, to understand these differences, it is necessary to understand conditions as they stood in each parish.

In the Second Church a 35-yr. pastorate came to an end just as the depression began. The minister who was called came with a distinctly different approach. The invested funds of the wealthier people fell off badly, and since these were on the whole people of elderly type, these funds were of tremendous importance to them as they looked forward to the coming years. My preaching had in it little of comfort, but stressed the rather radical social note. In the First Church everything was different. M——— was consolidating his ministry. The better off people were not elderly but in middle life and active—therefore less fearful of the future. M———'s preaching sounded the note of comfort and there was little in it to antagonize the socially conservative.

There were other factors also, of course. I mention these only to suggest how two case studies reveal widely differing conditions and widely differing effects.

I would not, then, be willing to generalize. My opinion is that the effects of the depression depend essentially upon the conditions and the factors entering into situations in addition to the factor of the depression. It takes theology, sociology and the personal relation between pastor and people. One of the least edifying things possible, I think, is to draw conclusions about the effects upon religion of one social situation without taking into consideration as of equal moment all the other situations and relationships explicitly.

The answer to these suggestions is that many case studies of churches in similar and unlike situations should be studied. The following proposed outline should be revised on the basis of its use in the study of a number of situations before adopting it as a plan of procedure.

The local church is the unit in which the support, loyalty, and participation of the individual members find expression and relationship to organized religion. In making the local church the unit of study, however, one must keep in mind the fact that the church is a part of a community. It is difficult to think of a church ending with its own membership. The local community of a church must be thought of as a part of the church. Except in cases where the membership of a church is virtually co-extensive with the community, the members are influenced by the attitudes of other people living in the vicinity. The local church, made up of persons with changing attitudes, may be thought of as the place where basic studies of what has happened during the depression could be made. It is interesting to see, however, to what extent the denomination becomes a significant unit and how the weight of the denomination as a whole pulls individual churches in a general direction. In studying the local church this denominational influence as well as the local community must be an object of concern.

There are a number of factors and forces which determine what happens to churches during a depression. These factors and forces vary from area to area, for example:

1. The wealth of the community and the occupations represented in the community.
2. The rate of reduction of the income during the depression, the extent of unemployment.
3. The cultural background, educational facilities and opportunities.
4. The types of religion represented in the community.
5. The conviction and general viewpoint and position of the minister and of prominent lay members of the church.
6. The nature of the religious organization itself—its type of organization and so on.
7. The nature of the local community might be described in census tract cities in terms of:
    a. Location in the city.
    b. Type of housing.
    c. Rental level.
    d. National elements.
    e. Educational level.

f. Age and sex distributions.
g. Mobility rate of populations.
h. Social forces in the community.

Churches are located in very different types of communities and share the fate of those communities. Selections might be made of downtown churches, of churches in rooming house areas, rescue missions among homeless men, churches in immigrant areas, churches in apartment house areas, churches in the various classes of suburbs, churches in various sized cities and towns, churches in the open country, and churches in mining areas. These rural churches could be selected from the many types of rural areas, corn, wheat, cotton, tobacco, fruit, dairying, etc.

A BRIEF OUTLINE OF A PLAN FOR STUDYING THE REACTIONS OF THE LOCAL CHURCH DURING THE DEPRESSION

In studying the relation of church to community one would need to study (a) the distance from the church of its membership, (b) the age groups in the church in relation to those of the community, (c) the economic status of church members in relation to the community, (d) the cooperation of the church with community agencies for social action or education, and (e) the program and activities of the church in relationship to the needs of the local community.

1. *Membership.* The membership of individual churches for past years may be secured from yearbooks. Quite a few churches are now keeping exact records by attendance. The increases and decreases of churches are related to many factors, such as, e.g., the popularity of a particular minister or the increase or decrease of a particular church constituency in a local community, competing churches, etc. Therefore, these factors must be kept in mind if an effort is to be made to assess the influence of the depression. Compare the regularity of attendance of those on relief with those not on relief.

2. *Finance.* In studying and charting the finances of the local church, one would seek to discover any significant differences of opinions which have arisen during the depression over the use of funds. Some churches had clashes over the use of funds for current expenses or for benevolences, especially in cases of church debts. Some clashes occurred over salary reduction. Some members objected to funds going for social action uses. A study of a number of cases would reveal the typical conflict situations.

A study of the finances of the local church would include a study from 1928 to the present time of the percentage of the budget devoted to staff, building debt, benevolences, maintenance, etc. These would need to be broken up into more specific items. These items may be charted in relationship to the church membership and attendance, where it is kept. One may put on the graph with these other items the pledges. The pledges may be broken up into the various sized gifts. Charts may be made which show what particular groups of givers have done throughout the depression. One must remember that a frequency distribution of gifts by size of contribution does not tell what a given group did through the depression. The fifty dollars per year group in 1932, for example, might include many who earlier gave one hundred dollars. This would help answer the question of the "democratization" of giving to churches.

The psychological aspects of giving are extremely difficult to explore. Yet some research efforts might not be unrewarded, even if the result of the investigation were merely a clarification rather than a verification of hypotheses. Particularly, it would be valuable to know whether inability to contribute caused a loss of pride which kept substantial numbers of people away from church.

3. *Control of Local Churches.* It has been assumed by some that the control of churches has moved into older hands. Has the depression speeded up a movement out of the church on the part of younger people? The statement is made that fewer young

people are interested in the church today than formerly—that they are far from being interested in who controls the church, that they are not interested in the church. Have there been shifts in the source of the new membership in terms of age groups?

4. *Relationship of Minister and Congregation.* Has there been conflict? Did the pastor feel that he should have moved but was unable to do so? When, if at all, was his salary reduced? Was his salary reduced without any request or resistance on his part? Was his salary reduced against his wishes. Were there any attitudes, favorable or unfavorable, toward the pastor?

5. *Sermons and Messages of the Minister.* (See chapter V, "The Message.") To what extent have changes in his theological position taken place due to the depression? To what extent have changes in his teachings regarding the rôle of the church in the social order taken place? If one desired to get a sample of opinions of many pastors quickly, rather than study one local church intensively, one might try the use of some such schedule as the following in questioning ministers:

THE CHURCH IN RELATION TO SOCIAL ISSUES[1]

A. Please check the statement below which best expresses your own personal conviction as to the rôle of social teaching in the church. If none of the following sentences is at all adequate to express your conviction, write your own statement in the space below—

1. —— The church has a duty to participate directly and as an institution in securing changes in the economic and political order.
2. —— The church may participate indirectly through its auxiliary or associated organizations and agencies in securing changes in the economic and political order.
3. —— The church should exercise its influence on politics and economic conditions by means of creating social-mindedness in the individual members of the congregation.
4. —— The church should devote itself to the salvation of men and not concern itself with changes in the economic and political order.
5. ——

[1] The author is indebted to Mr. Shirley Green for this outline

B. In general, would you say that the influential portion of your congregation holds the same position as you have indicated above as your own? ——. If not, in what direction does it differ?

C. Is there a significant difference in attitude between your adult membership and your young people with respect to the place of economic and political teachings in the church? ——. What difference?

Please indicate by a check:

1. Those which you favor personally.
2. Those which you discuss favorably in the pulpit.
3. Those which you personally oppose.
4. Those which your congregation would, in general, favor.
5. Those which your congregation would, in general, oppose.

(1) Favor personally	(2) Favor in pulpit	(3) Personally oppose	Social Issues	(4) Congregation favors	(5) Congregation opposes
——	——	——	Birth control	——	——
——	——	——	Civil service in government	——	——
——	——	——	Honest elections	——	——
——	——	——	Freedom of Speech	——	——
——	——	——	Socialized medicine	——	——
——	——	——	The right of labor to organize	——	——
——	——	——	Greater economic equality and justice	——	——
——	——	——	Growth of cooperatives	——	——
——	——	——	Abolition of profit system	——	——

At what points in the program of your church do teachings on economic and political issues find their major expressions? Indicate by a check:

1. Sunday morning sermon ——
2. Evening service —— Sunday or mid-week ——
3. Sunday-school (which departments?) ——
4. Forum ——
5. Young people's group ——
6. Women's groups ——
7. Men's groups ——
8. Special committee on social education ——
9. Special committee on social action ——

One has a right to be skeptical about the reliability and validity of such questionnaires. Yet if the proper rapport can be established—especially, at a conference in which a large number of ministers are met face to face by the research worker, and if anonymity can be guaranteed, the results might be a useful contribution to our knowledge. It may not be entirely too late to make such studies—but their validity will rapidly diminish as the worst of the depression fades farther and farther into the past.

6. *Changes in Members' Attitudes.*[2] There are implications throughout this monograph for the study of changes in the attitudes of individual members towards their churches. Attitude studies after the manner of Thurstone and Chave[3] would indicate the differences in attitudes in various groups, such as the officers and non-officers, and any other groups such as classes or women's societies. Such methods cannot be used to tell what the attitudes of any group was several years ago. In the case of future depressions, attitudes of various groups within a church might be studied at different periods of the depression, since it seems to be clear from casual observations that attitudes toward the church have been different at different periods in the depression.

---

[2] For bibliography see Murphy, Gardner and Barclay, Lois. *Experimental Social Psychology.* New York: Harper & Brothers. 1931; also Anderson, C. Arnold and Smith, T. Lynn. *Research in Social Psychology of Rural Life.* Bulletin No. 17. (Black, John D., Editor). New York: Social Science Research Council. June 1933

[3] Thurstone, L. L., and Chave, E. J. *The Measurement of Attitudes.* Chicago: University of Chicago Press. 1930

Appendix C

Notes on the Civic Functions of the Parish in Quebec in the Depression[1]

THE churches, both Catholic and Protestant, are more nearly "established" in the Province of Quebec than elsewhere in North America. The clergyman is, save for a few minor exceptions, the sole registrar of births (really baptisms) and marriages. Schools, while supported by taxation, are officially designated as Catholic or Protestant. Real property is listed as of Protestant or Catholic ownership. The school tax from each parcel is paid into the corresponding school fund. These funds are administered by separate Protestant and Catholic school boards. These and other similar arrangements rest on the constitutional rights granted to the French Catholics after the British conquest.

The local parish is consequently more than a "Communion of Saints." It is a civic institution. The French church warden is something of a local public official. The meeting of parish proprietors (freeholders) is something like a town meeting. Although financial responsibility lies with these lay officials, the parish priest actually has a great deal to say about the expenditure of money for churches, schools, hospitals, parish recreation halls, and even for roads and other local improvements. The financial obligations of the parish church are met by levies upon local property owned by the parishioners. A Catholic landholder is a parishioner by virtue of owning land in the parish, whether he is devout or not.

[1] Prepared for the author by Professor Everett C. Hughes of McGill University.

Care of the poor traditionally fell upon the parish. Government funds have been, and in many cases still are, allocated to the parish and to institutions maintained by various religious orders, e.g., orphanages, reformatories, asylums, hospitals.

With the growth of cities and the consequent unequal distribution of wealth and capable lay leadership among the city's parishes, it has become increasingly difficult for each parish to perform these civic functions independently. In Montreal and other sizable cities, city-wide Catholic school boards have been established to distribute schools equitably and to supervise instruction. School districts no longer coincide with parishes.

Some parishes are too poor to look after those in need of charity. The St. Vincent de Paul societies, organized into parish units under the direction of the parish priest, have been accustomed to looking after charity. But a diocesan direction is increasingly necessary to coordinate the efforts of parochial units. A further complication is that the population of mid-city parishes is so mobile that it is difficult to either determine parish membership or to recruit a stable lay leadership.

Nevertheless, when the depression changed "charity" into "relief of the unemployed" the parochial St. Vincent de Paul societies were entrusted with its distribution. The applicant for relief had to get right with parish officials. Eventually this system broke down. The officers of the St. Vincent de Paul societies were small local business men. In some cases they used their powers to compel those on relief to buy in their local stores. They also had relatives out of work, and were inclined to favor them. These irregularities were, in general, not wanton corruptions, but simply the result of the parochial spirit operating in a field too big for it.

These local parish officials also lacked entirely knowledge of the methods of investigation used by professional social workers and consequently were imposed upon by many of the unemployed. After much bickering, an investigation was undertaken of the relief system. The evils uncovered were whitewashed somewhat. Then relief was turned over to a secular city-wide commission, which deals with both Catholic and Protestant. The parishes were, on the whole, glad to be relieved of so troublesome a function. But the ward politicians are still complaining of the loss of patronage involved; under the parochial relief system, ward heeler and local relief officials could work together.

Early in the period of depression a number of French social agencies of the city of Montreal were grouped into a federation of French-Canadian charities, much like the older English Protestant Federation. This federation has grown and prospered, but has had the continued opposition of many parish priests, parochial societies, and religious orders. Its chief support has come from those French who have money and find it troublesome to be bothered by a multiplicity of parish organizations. There is also a group of French women who have something of the feminist spirit and wish to see the social problems of the city attacked in a big way. The bishop supports the federation, probably because he sees that the full resources of the community cannot be exploited by piecemeal, haphazard methods. The idea of having secularly trained professional social workers has not, however, made much headway.

Index

Activities, *see* Program and activities
Adams, Romanzo, 57
Adult Bible Class Magazine, The, 97
Adult education programs, 97, 108
Agricultural depression, effects, 131
Ames, Edward Scribner, 53, 56n, 63n
Anderson, C. Arnold, 145n
Announcements, change in content, 92
Anti-Liberalism movement, 54, 64
Anti-Secularism movement, 54
Attendance, church, 2, 12-16; factors responsible for fluctuations, 14; church schools: young people's conferences, 98; rural church, 134; *see also* Membership
Attitudes, toward social order, 31, 40, 46, 61, 68, 71, 73, 105, 143, 145; changing, of clergy, 39-42, 68, 83; questionnaire for study of, 42, 143
Aubrey, Edwin E., viii
Augustana Synod Lutheran, 120, 126

Babson, Roger W., 2, 14
Baptist churches, 6, 7, 20, 21, 81, 92, 120, 127, 132; organization of Laymen's Foreign Missions Inquiry, 100
Barclay, Lois, *see* Murphy, Gardner and Barclay, Lois
Barrett, C. B., 50n
Barth, Karl, 66
Barthianism, 52, 66, 74
Beecher, Lyman, 1
Benevolences, appropriations for, 27; of rural and village churches, 133; *see also* Missions
Bennett, John, quoted, 45
Berry, John, viii
Birth rate, relation to membership, 6, 8, 16, 93, 98
Black, John D., 145n
Bogoslovsky, Boris B., 82n
Bonded indebtedness, *see* Debts
Bower, William Clayton, viii, 97n, 98n
Brooklyn Church and Mission Federation, 104
Brunner, Edmund deS., 117n; and Lorge, Irving, *Rural Trends in Depression Years,* 13, 103n, 131, 134, 135, 136n, 137; and Kolb, J. H., . . . *Rural Social Trends,* 131n, 136n; *see also* Douglass, H. Paul and Brunner, E. deS.
Buchmanism, 54, 63
Budgets, family: church expenditures, 25
Building debts, 19, 20, 27
Business and religious cycles, relationship, 57
Business men, attitude toward relief and philanthropy, 105; attitude toward cooperatives, 115

Calvinistic-Lutheran theology, return to, 65, 67
Canada, relief situation, 30, 106, 147; schools, 106, 146; church organization, 146
Catholic church, *see* Roman Catholic church
Catholic Periodical Index, The, 75n

Catholic Rural Life Conference, 79
Census of Manufactures, 19
Census of Religious Bodies, 118, 130
Census tract cities, use of for studies, 86, 88
Central Conference of American Rabbis, 73n, 81
Chapin, F. Stuart and Queen, Stuart A., . . . *Social Work in the Depression,* 103n
Chapman, J. Wilbur, 1
Charities, *see* Relief and philanthropy
Chave, E. J., 91; *see also* Thurstone, L. L. and Chave, E. J.
Chicago, church studies, 15, 88, 118, 119; changes in church expenditures, 108
Chicago, University of, viii, 78
Chicago Congregational Union, viii, 15, 29, 88; study by, 118-30
Chicago Theological Seminary, viii, 15, 88; study by, 118-30
Christendom, 78
Christian Century, The, 75, 84, 85, 115; excerpt, 95
Christian Century Pulpit, The, 76, 84, 85
Christian Cooperative Fellowship in North America, 114
"Christian Cooperatives," 113
Christian Evangelist, The, 76
Christian schools of Reformed groups, 99
Christian Science, 56
Christian Standard, The, 76
Church, the term defined, vii; membership, 1-16, 24, 25, 67, 72, 93, 98, 117-37, 141; attendance, 2, 12-16, 98, 134; program and activities, 5, 14, 46, 49, 55, 64, 89-116; rural and village church, 13, 131-37; finances, 17-30, 98, 108, 110, 132, 142, 143, 146; grown institutional minded and introverted? 28; missions, 28, 29, 100-102, 110-13, 132; local church, 29, 55, 115, 138ff.; reduction in staff, 29, 38, 98; relief and philanthropy, 30, 51, 103-7; Canadian, 30, 106, 146-48; the clergy, 31-44, 50, 61, 68, 69, 70, 83, 87, 105, 106, 135, 143, 145, 146; attitudes toward social order, 31, 40, 46, 61, 68, 71, 73, 105, 143, 145; secularization, 45-58, 60, 63, 64, 105; educational function, 47, 48, 51, 55, 76, 96, 97, 106, 108, 112, 146; irrelevant nature of, 47; attitude toward government cooperation in work of, 50, 73, 107, 108, 111, 137; community church, 53, 102, 134; the message, 59-88, 143; dual function, 60; influence upon social order, 69; social creed of the churches, 73, 79; evangelism, 92; young people in, 98, 142; institutional churches and neighborhood houses, 107; regional and rural variations, 117-37; factors which determine effects of the depression, 140
Church and state, relationship, 73, 111
"Church member," concept of, 4
Church of Christ, 76
Church of Jesus Christ of Latter Day Saints, 106
Church schools, 97ff.; literature, 76, 97; attendance, 98; parochial schools, 99, 106, 146
Church union, 53, 102, 134
Cities, census tract: use of, for studies, 88
City areas, regional and situational variations, 130
City societies, 110-13
Clergy, changes among, 31-44; great Revivalists, 1; changing attitudes, 31, 39-42, 68, 83; attitude toward social order, 31, 40, 61, 145; rift between laity and, 31, 70, 143; changes in

number of ministers: of local preachers, 32; ministers admitted to full membership: number received on trial, 33; numbers retired, expelled, etc., 34; vertical and horizontal mobility, 35; seminary graduates, 37; salaries, 37, 143; duties, 38; sense of defeat, 41; questionnaire for study of attitudes, 42, 143; study of: statistical data on, 43; secularization of message, 50; adjustments to attitudes of members, 68, 69; preaching of ideals and radical doctrine, 70; subtle use of language, 83; facts about, as control data, 87; research on unemployment, 105; influence in behalf of relief, 106; in rural churches, 135; in local church, 143; functions of, in Canadian church, 146; message of, *see* Message of the church

Coe, George A., 96n

Colleges, religious control, 100

Communism, 3, 49, 53, 71

Community, relation of local church to, 140

Community church movement, 53, 102, 134

Community service, 103, 107

Congregational churches, 10, 13, 52n, 54, 92, 109, 124, 130; Commission on Church Attendance, 2; social action, 77, 80; pronouncements, 80

Congregational Union, Chicago, viii, 15, 29, 88; study by, 118-30

Conservatism, 20, 61, 64, 68ff.

. . . *Consumption in the Depression.* 114n

Contributions, 17-20, 21, 23; regional and denominational factors, 19; changes in size of, 24; for missions, 28, 29; local church, 142

Cooperatives, 113-15

Council for Social Action, 77, 80

Cummins, Ralph, viii, 109; quoted, 134, 136

Daily Vacation Bible Schools, 112

Danville, Ill., Nazarene group, 136

Debts, 17, 20-24, 27; building debts, 19, 20, 27; Roman Catholic churches, 30

Defeatism, 41, 52

Democratization, 24, 25

Denominations, variations in study of membership, 8; of contributions, 19; relation of growth to dominance, 15, 118; as factor in study of: membership and attendance, 16; finances, 19, 29; clergy, 43; secularization, 54; trends, 54; church message, 87; renewed theological orientation, 53; regional and rural variations, 117ff.; influence of, in study of local church, 140

Depression, relationship to interest in religion, 1ff.; supposed to drive men to God, 1, 95; produced by lack of spirituality, 2; articles on, in religious journals, 84; agricultural, 131; effects too varied for generalization, 138; factors which determine effects of, 140

Dewey, John, 57

Dialectic theology, 52, 66

Dickey, Paul, viii

Directors of religious education, 38, 39, 98

Disciples of Christ, 54, 76, 92, 125, 129, 130

Discussion groups, 97, 108

Divine, Father, 95

Douglass, Harlan Paul, 98, 102; and Brunner, E. deS., 117n

Economic order, *see* Social order; Depression

Economic pressure, influence upon message of church, 67ff.
Economics, cooperative movement, 113-15; making religion vital in realm of, 114
Education, 96-100; directors of religious education, 38, 39, 98; secularization of, 47, 48, 51, 55; church schools, 76, 97ff.; source material, 97; adult programs, 97, 108; young people's conferences, 98; parochial schools, 99, 106, 146; Canadian schools, 106, 146; church and government programs in New York City, 112
Emotional sects, growth of, 136
Emotional zeal, outlets for, 3, 71, 93
Encyclical Letter of Pope Leo XIII, 73n
English, M. N., *see* Hayward, P. H., *et al*
Ensminger, Douglas, *see* Sneed, Melvin W., and Ensminger, D.
Evangelical churches, 20
Evangelical Synod of North America, 8
Evangelism, 92-96
Evangelistic index, 10-12
Expenditures, 26-30; for congregational matters, 26, 27; for benevolences and other outside expenses, 27; as bases for study of program and activities, 91; for regular, as compared with institutional church work, 108

Fahs, Charles H., 29n
Family expenditure budgets, analysis of, 25
. . . *Family in the Depression,* 16n
Fascism, 3, 49
Federal Council of Churches of Christ in America, 14, 73n, 79, 94; pronouncements, 79; National Preaching Mission, 94
Filene, Edward A., quoted, 115
Finances, church, 17-30, 98; contributions, 17, 21; debts, 19, 20-24, 27, 30; changes in sources of income, 24; expenditures, 26, 108; salaries, 29, 37, 143; as basis for study of program and activities, 90; study of funds going into "institutional" work, 108; Methodist City Society funds, 110; rural and village churches, 132; local church, 142; Canadian church, 146
Finney, Charles G., 1
Foreign missions, *see* Missions
Forums, 97, 108
Four-Square Gospel, 137
French social agencies, Montreal, 148
Fry, C. Luther, 6n, 137n; quoted, 132; *The U. S. Looks at Its Churches,* 118
Fundamentalism, 54
Fundamentalist groups, membership, 7, 8

Gaddis, M. E., 2n, 94n
Germany, dialectic theology, 52, 66
Gibson, George M., "Worship and Theology," excerpts, 65
Giersbach, Marion, viii
Gifts, *see* Contributions
God, association with depressions, 1, 95; conceptions of, 66, 67
Good Neighbor League, 73
Goodwin plan, 22
Government, cooperation in community and recreational work of churches, 50, 107, 108, 111, 137; idealistic social program, 73; church's fear of following lead of, 73, 108
Graduates of seminaries, placements, 37
Greene, Ellen Tweedy, viii
Greene, Shirley, viii, 143n
Guthrie, Ernest Graham, viii

Harkness, Georgia, 3n
Hartshorne, Hugh: and Stearns, Helen R. and Uphaus, W., 96n
Hayward, P. H., *et al,* 96n
Health, relation of religion to, 56; Illinois data, 119
Hobson, J. A., 3n
Hocking, W. E., 101n
Holt, Arthur E., viii, 80, 99, 106n
Holyoake, G. J., 49
Home missions, *see* Missions
Hughes, Everett C., 30, 146n
Humanism, 64

Illinois, church membership study, 15; distribution of church membership by areas *with maps,* 118-30; union movements, 134
Illinois Regional Planning Association, 119
Income, national, 17, 18
Income sources, church, 17-20; changes in, 24-26
Indexes for membership measurement, 10
Institute of Social and Religious Research, 100
Institutional churches, 107-10
International Council of Religious Education, 100n
International Missionary Council, 49

Jaffe, A. J., 16n
Jewish charities, 104
Jewish synagogues, factors causing changes in, 8, 9; finances, 30
Jews, vii, social ideals, 73n, 82; literature, 77
Johnson, F. Ernest, 56, 103n
Jones, Rufus M., 49
Journal of Religion, 78
Journals, religious, 75-78, 84-86

Kagawa, Toyohiko, 114
Kallen, Horace M., 115
"Kingdom of God Fellowship," 114
Kolb, J. H., *see* Brunner, E. deS. and Kolb, J. H.
Kone, Marilee, viii
Krueger, Ernest T., quoted, 71

Landis, Benson Y., 3n
Language, religious, 63, 64, 65, 73, 83
Laymen's Foreign Missions Inquiry, 100, 101, 102
Lazarsfeld, Paul F., *see* Stouffer, Samuel A., and Lazarsfeld, P. F.
League for Social Justice, 71
Leo XIII, Pope, 73n
Liberalism, 20, 52, 64, 70, 73, *see also* Anti-Liberalism
Literature, religious, 75-78, 97
Local church, dependence on regional or national organizations, 29; secularization in, 55; study of, 115, 138-45; relation to community, 140; membership, 141; control of: finances, 142; minister: message, 143; members' attitudes, 143, 145
"Local preachers," 32
Long, Huey, 3
Lorge, Irving, *see* Brunner, E. deS. and Lorge, Irving
Lutheran church, 7, 8, 20, 81, 92, 99, 126
Lynd, Robert S., and Helen M., *Middletown in Transition,* 42, 89, 93

McCullough, Charles J., 14
McGiffert, Arthur Cushman, Jr., viii
McGowan, R. A., 79
MacMurray, John, 53n
Manufactures, Census of, 19
Maps, Illinois counties: church membership in, 121-128

Maurer, Heinrich H., 117n
May, Mark A., *et al,* 37n, 74n
Medland, Margaret, viii
Membership, 1-16; attendance, 2, 12-16, 98, 134; methods of enumerating; quantitative changes; concept of "church member," 4; participation in activities of church, 5; regional changes, 6; relation to birth rate, 6, 8, 16, 93, 98; relative constancy of denominational groups, 8; evangelistic and net gains indexes, 10; qualitative changes, 12; factors responsible for fluctuations, 14; relation of migration to, 15; democratization in, 24, 25; was message of church influenced by economic conditions of? 67; by political attitudes of? 72; regional and rural variations, 117-37; in Illinois, 118; local church, 141
Message of the church, 59-88; conception of, 59; personal and social aspects, 60; questions and hypotheses on the effects of depression: whether message more social or personal, 62; more secular or sacred: whether secularization speeded up, 63; movement away from liberalism, 64; development of German dialectic theology in U.S., 66; whether influenced by economic conditions of members, 67; by political attitudes of members, 72; effects of depression on seminary teaching, 74; sources of data, 74; religious journals, 75; pronouncements and resolutions, 78; research, 82; background factors, 86; in local church, 143
Methodist churches, 7, 20, 23, 70, 130; pronouncements, 80; city missions, 110-13
Methodist City Society of New York, 110-13
Methodist Episcopal church, 23, 32n, 37, 43, 92, 109, 122, 129
Methodist Episcopal Church South, 23
Methodist Youth, National Council of, 80
. . . *Migration in the Depression,* 15n, 16n
Migration, relationship of, to membership, 15, 130
Miller, Francis P., *see* Niebuhr, H. Richard, *et al*
Mills, Fay B., 1
Ministers, great Revivalists, 1; effective: changes in number and status of, 32-44; *see also* Clergy
Minsky, Louis, 81
Missions, changing attitude toward, 28; contributions for, 28, 29; foreign missions, 100-102; city societies: Methodist program in New York, 110-13; rural churches, 132
Missouri, rural churches, 134, 136
Missouri Synod Lutheran Church, 8, 20, 120
Modern Missions Movement, 101
Montreal, relief situation, 106, 148; schools, 147
Moody Bible Institute Monthly, The, 84, 85
Mormons, Church Security Program, 106
Morrison, Charles Clayton, 76, 92n
Mortgages, *see* Debts
"Movement for World Christianity, A," 101, 102
Moyle, Henry D., 106; quoted, 107
Murphy, Gardner, and Barclay, Lois, 145n
Murray, Gilbert, *Five Stages of Greek Religion,* 54
Myers, Harry S., 18

National Catholic Welfare Conference, 73n, 79
National Committee of the Modern Missions Movement, 101

National Council of Methodist Youth, 80
National Preaching Mission, 93, 94
Nazarenes, 136
"Near religious movements" as outlet for emotional zeal, 3, 71
Negro churches, membership, 7
Neighborhood houses, 107-10
Neo-Calvinism, 52, 54, 55
Net gains index, 10-12
New Deal, 3; attitudes toward, 72, 73; social program, 73; *see also* Government
New York City Society, Methodist Episcopal Church, 110-13
New York Times, 75
Newell, Frederick B., 105n; quoted, 110-13
Newspapers, religious data in, 75; attitude toward church charities, 104, 105
Newton's Law of Action and Reaction, 2
Niebuhr, H. Richard, *et al,* 49n
Niebuhr, Reinhold, and MacMurray, John, *A Creative Society,* 53n; *Reflections on the End of an Era,* 52
Northern Baptist Church, 127
Norton, John K., 96n
Notestein, Frank W., 16n

Ogburn, William F., 26
Oldham, J. H., 64n
Oxford Group Movement, 62

Parish, Canadian, 146
Parochial schools, 99; in Canada, 106, 146
Pauck, Wilhelm, *see* Niebuhr, H. Richard, *et al*
Pentecostal group, 136
Personal aspects of message, 60, 62
Peterson, Audrey, viii
Philanthropy, *see* Relief and philanthropy
Pius XI, Pope, 73n, 79; "Reconstructing the Social Order," 78
Political affiliation, effects of, 72, 87
Political and social order, *see* Social order
Population movements, effect upon membership, 15; urban, 130
Post liberals, 67n
"Preachers, local," 32
Preaching, as function of church, 59; at variance with practice, 70; *see also* Message
Preaching Mission, 93
Presbyterian Advance-Tribune, The, 84, 86
Presbyterian Church of the U.S.A., 7, 15, 20, 36, 37, 54, 92, 115, 123, 129, 130, 132; membership index, 10; pronouncements, 81; neighborhood houses, 109
Priests, in Canada, 146; *see also* Clergy
Program and activities, 89-116; classification of participation in, 5, 14; missions, 28, 29, 100-102, 110-13, 132; relief and philanthropy, 30, 51, 103-7; taken over by larger community, 46, 49, 55, 64; educational work, 47, 48, 51, 55, 76, 96, 97, 106, 108, 112, 146; government participation in, 50, 73, 107, 108, 111, 137; church union, 53, 102, 134; outline for study of, 90; the worship service, 91; evangelism, 92; social and community service, 103, 107; institutional churches: neighborhood houses, 107; city societies, 110; relation between church and cooperatives, 113; survey of local churches, 115
Pronouncements and resolutions, 73n, 78-82; Jewish, 73n, 81; Roman

Catholic, 78; Federal Council of Churches of Christ in America, 79; Congregational-Christian: Methodist, 80; Presbyterian: other groups, 81
Property debts, 19, 20, 27; *see also* Debts
Protestant churches, vii, 5ff.
Protestant Episcopal Church, 27, 92, 93, 132
Quebec, churches: relief, 146-48
Queen, Stuart A., *see* Chapin, F. Stuart, and Queen, S. A.
Questionnaire, for study of attitudes, 42; church in relation to social issues, 143

Rabbinical Assembly of America, 73n
Radical doctrine, preaching of, 70
"Reconstructing the Social Order," 73n, 78, 79
Recreational work, 107
Reform, limitations of, 52, 70
Reformation theology, return to, 67
Reformed church, 20
Reformed groups, Christian schools, 99
Regional variations, in church membership, 6, 13, 15, 117-37; contributions, 19, 26; in study of church finances, 19, 30; in the study of the clergy, 43; in study of secularization, 55; in study of message, 87; in study of program and activities, 116
Relief and philanthropy, 103-7; Canadian situation, 30, 106, 147; secularization of, 51; Protestant, compared with Catholic and Jewish organization, 104; Mormon, 106
. . . *Relief Policies in the Depression,* 103n
Religion, relationship to periods of depression, 1ff.; lack of, as cause of depressions, 2; outlets for emotional zeal, 3, 71; renewed theological orientation, 52, 53; *see also* Church; Message of the Church: Secularization
Religious and business cycles, relationship, 57
Religious Bodies, Census of, 118, 130
Religious education, *see* Education
Religious Education Association, 100n
Religious journals, 75-78, 84-86
Research suggestions, *passim;* church membership and attendance, 1-16; membership, 4; attendance, 12; factors to be considered, 14; church finances, 17-30; contributions, 17; debts, 20; changes in income, 24; expenditures, 26; the clergy, 31-44; number, 32; vertical and horizontal mobility, 35; seminary graduates: salaries, 37; duties, 38; changes in attitudes, 39; suggested questionnaire, 42; factors to be controlled, 43; secularization, 45-58; frame of reference for study, 48; subdivision of problem, 53; the message, 59-88; questions and hypotheses on effects of the depression, 62; teaching in seminaries and theological schools: sources of data, 74; example of study of message, 84; background factors to be considered, 86; program and activities, 89-116; worship service, 91; evangelism, 92; educational work, 96; foreign missions, 100; church union, 102; philanthropy, relief, and social and community service, 103; institutional churches and neighborhood houses, 107; city societies, 110; cooperatives, 113; regional and rural variations, 117-137; rural churches, 131; study of local church, 138-145: factors and forces which determine effects of the depression, 140; outline of plan of study, 141
Resolutions, *see* Pronouncements and Resolutions
Restoration Journal, The, 76

Re-Thinking Missions, 67, 101
Revivalists and depressions of the past, 1
Revivals, 1, 92-96
Ritual, 92
Riverside Church, New York, 108
Robertson, H. M., 3n
Robinson, Gilbert K., viii, 9, 16n, 109
Roman Catholic church, vii, 5, 7, 30, 75, 77, 92, 93, 99, 120, 121; pronouncements, 73n, 78; parochial schools, 99, 106, 146; charities and relief, 104, 106; in Canada, 146-48
Roosevelt, Franklin D., 3, 73, 95
Rural and village church, 131-37; attendance, 13; financial trend, 132; benevolence giving, 133; attendance: union movements, 134; clergy, 135; villageward trend, 136; emotional sects, 136
. . . *Rural Life in the Depression*, 131
Rural variations in church membership, 117ff.

Sacred nature of message, 63
St. Vincent de Paul societies, 147
Salaries, 29, 36, 37-38, 143
Sanderson, Dwight, . . . *Rural Life in the Depression*, 131
Schattenmann, Johannes, 95
Schools, *see* Church schools
Secular order, defined, 45
Secularism, emotional zeal going into, 3, 71
Secularization, 45-58, 64, 105; meaning of term, 45; of education, 47, 48, 51, 55; frame of reference for study of, 48; factors which may have speeded up secularization, 49; or slowed it down, 51; subdivision, 53; by size and nature of unit, 54; by study of functions, 55; a factor in teachings of church, 60; of message, 63
Security of the person, 71
Seminaries, graduates, 37; conservative position, 64; teaching in, 74
Sermons, recorded in journals and newspapers, 75ff.; change in content, 92; *see also* Message
Share-Your-Wealth Club, 71
Smith, T. Lynn, 145n
Sneed, Melvin W., and Ensminger, Douglas, *The Rural Church in Missouri*, 94n, 135, 136; excerpt, 134
Social Action, 77, 80
Social Action, Council for, 52n, 77, 80, 142
Social aspects of message, 60, 62
Social creeds of the churches, correspondence between government program and, 73; adopted, 79
Social Gospel movement, 54; ideas of God and man, 66
Social Ideals, Jewish, 73n, 82
Social order, attitudes toward, 1, 31, 40, 61, 68, 71, 73, 105, 143, 145; chasm between church and, 46; influence of church upon, 69
Social security program of Mormons, 106
Social service, 103
Social service and reform, activities of Congregationalists, 77; pronouncement of Federal Council of Churches . . ., 79
"Social Service Party," 105
. . . *Social Work in the Depression*, 103n
Socialism, 71
Source data, limitations, 43; on church message, 74-82; religious journals, 75; pronouncements and resolutions, 78; *see also* Research suggestions
Southern Baptist Church, 128
Spengler, Oswald, *Decline of the West*, 54
Spinka, Matthew, 3n
Spirituality, *see* Religion

Staff, reduction in, 29, 38, 98; salaries, 29
State and church, relationship, 73, 111
Statistical data, from church reports, limitations, 43
Stearns, Helen R., *see* Hartshorne, Hugh and Stearns, Helen R. and Uphaus, W.
Stelzle, Charles, 73n
Stock, Harry Thomas, 99
Stouffer, Samuel A. and Lazarsfeld, Paul F., . . . *The Family in the Depression,* 16n
Sunday schools, *see* Church schools
Supplementary Series to Re-Thinking Missions, 100, 101
Sweet, William Warren, 54n

Tawney, R. H., 3n
Teaching, as function of church, 59; in Theological schools, 74; *see also* Education: Message
Theological schools and seminaries, placement of graduates, 37; conservative position, 64; teaching in, 74
Theological Seminary, Chicago, viii, 15, 88; study by, 118-30
Theology, dialectic, 52, 66
Thompson, Warren E., viii
Thompson, Warren S., . . . *Migration in the Depression,* 15n, 16n
Thurstone, L. L. and Chave, E. J., 145
Tibbetts, Norris, 102n
Time, 94
Times, New York, 75
Titus, P. M., viii
Totalitarian state, 49, 53, 64, 73
Townsend Plan, 3, 71
Troyer, Lewis, viii, quoted, 84-86

Umbeck, Sharvy, viii
Union movements, 53, 102, 134
Union of American Hebrew Congregations, 73n
Union Theological Seminary, 64
Uphaus, W., *see* Hartshorne, Hugh and Stearns, Helen R. and Uphaus, W.
Urban areas, regional and situational variations, 130

Vaile, Roland S., . . . *Consumption in the Depression,* 114n
Versteeg, John M., 62
Village church, *see* Rural and village church
Vogt, Von Ogden, 56n
Volunteers, use of, 38

Waldo, Alfred F., 1n
Wallace, Henry C., 3, 73, 95
Webber, Herman C., 7, 57n, 103n; cited, 10-12
Weber, Max, 3n
Wesley, John, 63
White, R. Clyde and Mary K., . . . *Relief Policies in the Depression,* 103n
Wilson, P. W., 2
Works Progress Administration, 108, 112
World Christianity: A Digest, 101
Worship service, 91

Young people, movement out of church, 142
Young people's conferences, 98

Studies in the Social Aspects of the Depression

AN ARNO PRESS/NEW YORK TIMES COLLECTION

Chapin, F. Stuart and Stuart A. Queen.
Research Memorandum on Social Work in the Depression. 1937.

Collins, Selwyn D. and Clark Tibbitts.
Research Memorandum on Social Aspects of Health in the Depression. 1937.

The Educational Policies Commission.
Research Memorandum on Education in the Depression. 1937.

Kincheloe, Samuel C.
Research Memorandum on Religion in the Depression. 1937.

Sanderson, Dwight.
Research Memorandum on Rural Life in the Depression. 1937.

Sellin, Thorsten.
Research Memorandum on Crime in the Depression. 1937.

Steiner, Jesse F.
Research Memorandum on Recreation in the Depression. 1937.

Stouffer, Samuel A. and Paul F. Lazarsfeld.
Research Memorandum on the Family in the Depression. 1937.

Thompson, Warren S.
Research Memorandum on Internal Migration in the Depression. 1937.

Vaile, Roland S.
Research Memorandum on Social Aspects of Consumption in the Depression. 1937.

Waples, Douglas.
Research Memorandum on Social Aspects of Reading in the Depression. 1937.

White, R. Clyde and Mary K. White.
Research Memorandum on Social Aspects of Relief Policies in the Depression. 1937.

Young, Donald.
Research Memorandum on Minority Peoples in the Depression. 1937.